LAUREL EDITION

The lives of the Saints were dedicated to a two-fold purpose: first to propagate the good news of the Messiah; second, to follow in their Master's footsteps. Miss Simon's penetrating narrative tells the dramatic and often moving story of these early heroes of the Christian faith. The book is richly illustrated with photographs of icons, mosaics, and catacomb reliefs as well as the works of later artists.

EDITH SIMON is well known as a writer of novels and of histories, among them *The Making of Frederick the Great, The Piebald Standard* and *The Reformation.*

D1546105

PAGEANT OF HISTORY SERIES

THE SAINTS

Edith Simon

Published by
Dell Publishing Co., Inc.
750 Third Avenue
New York, New York 10017

Manufactured in the United States of America
First Laurel printing—November 1971

Contents

Acknowledgements

The author and publishers would like to thank the people and institutions below for permission to reproduce the photographs on the pages mentioned before their names.

28, 48, 92, Alinari; 46, (top), 78/79, Anderson; Bayerisches National-museum; 27 (top and bottom), 60(right), 76, 77, 89, 90, 109, British Museum; 73, Coptic Museum, Cairo (photo W. Forman); 57, Fitz-william Museum, Cambridge; 26 (bottom), Museo Capitolino; 59, 61 (left), 80 (top and bottom), 91 (top and bottom), 110 (top and centre), 112, André Held; 26 (top), 62 ,63 (top and bottom), 62/63, 64, 74 (top and bottom), 75, 111, Norwich Castle Museum; 110 (bottom), Pont. Comm. di Arch. Sacra; 60, Hans Sibbelee; 25, Tretiakov Gallery; 45, 58, Victoria and Albert Museum.

The pictures from the Norwich Castle Museum are watercolours, executed in the nineteenth century by C. J. W. Winter, of fifteenth-century screen or glass paintings in Norfolk churches.

All line-drawings, unless otherwise specified in the caption, were photographed from William Caxton's *Golden Legend* (1493) by John Freeman & Co. at the British Museum.

1

A D 30

In the time of Jesus the country of Palestine was a part of the Roman commonwealth, under which all native religions were as far as possible tolerated. The central administration of the Empire did not care how many different provincial deities were venerated so long as those deities ceded their allegiance to the Roman pantheon which represented the state. Indeed Rome was always willing to give such deities immigrant status in the City itself, so that resident devotees might have somewhere to worship. Since, as so often, a period of material affluence had given rise to a certain spiritual boredom among the citizenry of Rome, foreign gods were positively welcome. Romans liked to dabble in the various exotic cults, partly from curiosity and partly in the hope of something new and tonic. Meanwhile it was understood that everyone, including subject populations, paid formal homage to Jupiter Capitolinus, the head of the Latin gods, who in any case was not essentially different from his opposite numbers elsewhere.

The abstract monotheism of the Jews made them an exception. The God of the Jews was not the head of a college of divinities but reigned entirely alone; he was more than a kind of supernatural paramount chieftain who would be satisfied with gestures of submission to an arbitrary, illogical, and quite unsystematic rule. The Jewish God was identified with the whole spirit and destiny of his people, demanding their undivided interest, and he made it a prime condition of rapport that no other gods whatsoever were to be recognised. Permeated through and through with consciousness of the divine being, in which consciousness they saw the entire meaning of existence, the Jews were fanatical theocrats, and cleaved to their invisible, omnipresent Lord through thick and thin. For this reason it had proved too troublesome to insist on the usual formalities of homage to the Roman gods, with them. Hypersensitive as they were in the religious sphere, so long as in this sphere they were left alone, the Jews could be made to function as useful members of the imperial commonwealth, particularly as semi-colonists in other parts of the world.

For the Jews were accustomed to such a role. Their small country, which was the geographical intersecting point of many standard routes of trade and conquest, had been frequently overrun and annexed by alien powers, who had time and again transplanted whole Jewish communities into the victors' territories, so that already there were Jews of many nations. Jerusalem remained the centre of their spiritual orientation, much as Rome was the hub of an equally heterogeneous, albeit concrete, Empire.

Besides the fact that thus the Jews had reliable contacts everywhere, an important factor of their usefulness was that they could more or less all read and write. They were called the People of the Book. Their entire lives were governed by a corpus of sacred writings, which were not merely liturgical and hieratic, but embodied a comprehensive network of rules and regulations for every aspect of conduct, whether ethical or practical. The sacred writings therefore had to be accessible to all.

This same incentive to literacy, however, offset the potential attractions of the Jewish faith to others. While that faith offered the boon of immortality in return for perfect observance of the divine decrees, and while it appealed to anybody with a cogitative turn of mind, the rules and regulations were too many – especially, as is the way of law, in point of prohibitions – for comfort. Also, to be a Jew, a man had to be circumcised. The foreskin was the one indispensable initiation fee to the congregation of Jewry: a painful and irrevocable form of sacrifice, which repelled many would-be proselytes. Some who could not bring themselves to take this step formed a looser, as it were associate attachment to various Jewish communities within the Empire, by which they participated in the spiritual-intellectual benefits without the final, crowning guarantee of belonging to the elect who were due to inherit the earth as well as life everlasting.

Meanwhile the Law by which they lived had proved in some degree disadvantageous to the spiritual welfare of the Jews themselves. Or so some sections of them thought. Insensibly there had come into being a confusion of ideas, whereby it was forgotten that the Law was designed as an aid to rectitude, not an end in itself. Correct observance was so manifold and took up so much time that the majority of simpler souls had pardonably arrived at the tacit conclusion that such outward obedience was all that mattered. Prayer, probity, charity, and moral soundness in general had become regarded as a species of tax payable to the deity, rather than means of communion with the deity. The ideal, organic relationship between man and god was threatening to turn into just such a fortuitous and inconsequential one as characterised the pagan creeds. Abstract monotheism too had become very much externalised.

This state of affairs was what Jesus set out to remedy. He was neither the first nor the only contemporary Jewish thinker wishing to purge, refresh, or develop Judaism – as had after all been the object of successive prophets of the past. Within the overall fold of orthodoxy there were, also, many sectary sub-groups. Any group of ten men or upwards was entitled to form a synagogue or religious community. Jesus and his disciples were thirteen in all. But they were itinerant preachers, and had neither need nor desire for a particular assembly place of their own. On the contrary, it was the sovereign burden of the leader's message that God must be served in the spirit, by the spirit, for the spirit; externals were secondary, if not wholly irrelevant.

This does not mean that they did not attend places of worship wherever they happened to be at the time, nor continue to observe the Law in which they had been brought up and which constituted the only climate they knew. They treated custom for what it was, a social more than an intrinsically religious matter, and accordingly eschewed a pointless rigidity. It was not until the last stage of his ministry that Jesus completely cast the Law aside.

Jesus was a teacher, an educator. His foremost aim was to reach the ordinary people – instead of preaching, in a manner, to the converted: that is, to those already learned and engrossed in deeper religious thought. He was at pains to render what, when all is said, were complex and often esoteric concepts, in language and imagery assimilable by the simplest minds. It was they who particularly needed enlightening as to the misleading courses into which religion had fallen and which so far from fulfilling the covenant between God and Abraham were liable utterly to frustrate it. His divine mandate was attested by miracles of a humanitarian nature, serving also as object lessons of disinterested

Sexta etas mūdi

IHesus xp̄us dei filiꝰ saluator ⁊ redēptor noster. Imperii Augusti cesaris qui tuz orbi impitabat anno q̄dragesimoscēdo. Cirino tuz preside: vniuerso orbe pacato i bethleem iude nascit' que Maria virgo angelo annūciāte ex spūsancto cōcepit ⁊ pepit ad abolendā humani generis labē ꝓpter primor inobediētiā cōtractā. Qui nascēdo viuēdo moriēdo resuscitando ⁊ in celū ascēdēdo vt deū se ostēderet multa ⁊ inaudita miracula fecit. Quor primū est qd tam mirabilit natus sit. Et angeli in celo cantauerunt Gloria in excelsis deo. ac pastoribus gaudiū magnū angeli euangelizauerūt dicētes natū esse mūdi saluatorē. Deinde octaua die delatꝰ fuit in templū circūcisionis grā: ⁊ ihesus appellatꝰ. Postea tredecima die magi ad eū adorandū tribꝰ muneribꝰ in syriā pretexerūt: stella duce. Hūc deinde puerulū die q̄dragesimo mater in tēplū detulit. quē symon vir iustus in vlnis suscipiēs saluatorē ꝓfitēdo ait. Nunc dimittis seruū tuū dn̄e in pace ⁊c̄. Inde post quietē Joseph ab angelo admonitꝰ vt eū cū matre in egyptū trāsferret cu futurū esset vt Herodes pueros occideret. Ibi vsq ad obitū herodis cōmoratus. Inde in ciuitate nazareth habitare cepit: ꝓpter quod nazarenus appellatꝰ fuit. Cetera ex familiarissima euāgelii historia patēt.

Ihꝰ xꝰ nasci aº m̄di 4200

Procuratores Judee

Archelaus

Componius

Marcus

Annius

Valerius

Pontius pilatus

ARchelaꝰ magni herodis filiꝰ p̄re sublato regnāt annis. 9. Ipsiuz augustꝰ ob p̄ris amorē cuz ceteris fratribꝰ maxio sp honore ꝓsecutꝰ fuit. Tandē accusatꝰ ab augusto apud viennā allobrogū ciuitatē relegatꝰ fuit. ⁊ fines eiꝰ in ꝓuīciā redacti sunt.

CHristus ih̄s agēs duodecimū annū cū parētibꝰ ad diē festū celebrādum hierosolimā de more petiit. Ibiq i tēplo duz inter sacre legis doctores nexus ambiguos solueret nō dc̄: s3 admirāde indolis puer ab eis creditꝰ est: parētes v̄o inde abeuntes cū puer subseq nō viderēt solicitudine pleni ad tēplū redeunt: eūq inter sacre legis doctores sciscitātē iuenerunt. a q̄bus bene monitꝰ in patriaz cuz eisdē reuersus est. ⁊ subditus fuit illis.

COmponiꝰ q̄ cirini collega fuit ab augusto: pꝰ archelauz mittit ꝓcurator.

MArcus cōponio romam reuerso successit. sub quo salome soror herodis defuncta fuit.

ANniꝰ ruffus successit marco. sb q̄ moritur augustꝰ dn̄o. 15. annum agente.

DOminꝰ ih̄s cuz. 30. annor etatis esset ad apiendaz vite eterne ianuaz. i iordanis alueo se a iohe baptizari voluit: statimq vox e celo intonuit. Hic est filiꝰ meꝰ ⁊c̄. ipm audite. ⁊ spiritꝰ sanctꝰ in modū columbe sup cuz mansit. deinde i desertuz ductꝰ. 40. diebꝰ ⁊ noctibꝰ ieiunauit: ⁊ postea esuriit. Inde q3 supatis diaboli tētatiōibꝰ. Cum postea in templum venisset deo vēdentes ⁊ ementes eiecit ⁊c̄.

VAleriꝰ romanꝰ ex illustri graccor familia natꝰ āno p̄mo impii Tiberii cesaris ab eo ꝓcurator pꝰ anniū ruffū i iudeā mittit: q̄ mg̃ratu suscepto p̄mꝰ apd iudeos pōtificatū vēdere cepit. ⁊ p̄fuit annis. 9.

PIlatꝰ natione gallꝰ ex lugduno vrbe natꝰ vir callidꝰ ⁊ facinorosus. Anno 13. impii Tiberii ce. valerio gracco p̄dicto abrogato. iudee ꝓcurator a cesare designatus: p̄fuit ānis. 10. Is suo ingenio iudeor vesaniā suppssit: ⁊ postmodū eor suggestione ihm cruci affixit. deinde sibi timens de eiꝰ doctrina morteq admonere tiberiuz curauit: q̄ eū in deos referēdū cēsuit: senatꝰ vetuit qꝛ nō ad se p̄iꝰ s3 ad tiberiuz scpsisset: inde ꝓpter iudeor accusatiōes ab officio amotꝰ: apd lugdunū orꝰ sui ciuitatē ꝑpetuo exilio i opprobriū gētis sue relegatus fuit: ⁊ malo fine periit.

Aº m̄di 4211. Aº x̄. 12.

Aº m̄di 4229. Aº x̄. 30.

Aº m̄di 4233. Aº x̄. 34.

The sixth stage of the World: the Age of Christ

love and goodness. But above all it was what he had to say, and the convincing clarity of the way he said it, which got home. (That his teaching would not prove equally plain to future generations was understandable – seeing that he addressed himself to his coevals in a rather specialised culture and associative idiom.) Possessed of an evidently most impressive and winning personality, he made considerable headway. In a small country, at a time of comparatively small populations and small popular initiative, he drew thousands under his influence; and his term of public teaching covered only three years altogether.

As no sphere of human endeavour exists in isolation, there were complications to this at first glance straightforward, unpolitical reform programme. For one thing, in a theocratic society nothing could in fact be less unpolitical than theology. Where there is orthodoxy, there is inevitable vigilance against heresy. Where there is emphasis on purity, there is always a corresponding terror of defilement. Where there is a strong national consciousness, there is chronic danger of rebellion against any foreign occupying power, however lenient. Occupation as such squared with oppression. Israel with its transcending belief of holding the monopoly of spiritual truth was less than any other nation inclined to rest quiescent in dependence: yet such dependence had mostly been its lot over the centuries. This was where the Messianic idea came in.

The historic misfortunes of Israel were explained as God's punishment upon the nation for its shortcomings in the past, to be repealed some day by the agency of an Anointed One who would redeem the people, reinstate them as the Lord's elect, and so lead them to the promised, ultimate triumph. Messiah and Christ were words respectively derived from the Hebrew and the Greek for 'the Anointed', and the belief that such a one must come was the vital hope and fuel which kept Jewry going, braced, fortified against resignation, in a perpetual state of expectancy.

There were different schools of thought as to the guise in which the Anointed Redeemer would appear. Some anticipated a royal king, some a modern prophet; there were also mystical predictions of a 'Suffering Servant' and sacrificial lamb in human shape, recalling again the covenant with Abraham. In so vast and mixed a canon as the sacred books, scriptural chapter and verse were to be found for each of these interpretations. The most popular one, cherished on the broadest level, was of course the conception of the typical folk hero, a conquering prince who would break all worldly bondage while he was about it. Accordingly, political revolt in Judaea usually came under the banner of the Messiah. Several such had occurred in recent memory, and had been crushed, with the false Messiahs exposed as they were put to death and thus shown to be powerless. The thrilling title of Messiah had begun to carry unhealthy overtones, of both sedition and blasphemy.

When it began to be said of Jesus that he was the Anointed One, both the religious Establishment and the temporal authorities were alerted, all the more so in view of his growing popular following. When finally he himself admitted to the title, the challenge could not be ignored, especially as he deliberately went to Jerusalem for the season of Passover, during which Jews from all over the world came to perform their devotions at the Temple which was their supreme sanctuary.

On the orders of the Jewish Council Jesus was arrested, and tried and convicted by an ecclesiastical court for blasphemy and subversion: the man actually called himself the Son of God. The penalty was death, a verdict which had to be ratified by the civil power. The Roman governor was told that here was another dangerous trouble-maker, self-styled 'King of the Jews', and though he was himself favourably impressed by the accused he at length committed him to execution.

Although primarily determined by Jews, the execution was carried out, as in all such cases, by soldiers of the Roman garrison, and took the Roman form of crucifixion, which not only was shameful but, for orthodox Jewish believers, entailed the destruction of the soul as well as of the body. Crosses with condemned malefactors hung upon them were as familiar a sight in Roman dominions as gibbets were to be throughout mediaeval Europe. Jewish eccentric enthusiasts or, for that matter, pretenders to sovereignty, were two a penny. There was nothing inordinately remarkable about the end of this one, except that it coincided with what looked like an eclipse and an earthquake in which the fabric of the Temple, that central shrine of Israel, was badly damaged. Jesus himself, who had foreseen and invited his own martyrdom, appeared to lose heart at the last, and died with a terrible cry of despair, defeated. All save one of his disciples had deserted him, lying low in fear of contamination by association; otherwise there were only his mother and a few other women – socially and spiritually negligible entities – to attend him in death.

Death occurred unusually soon. Private arrangements had been made for the body so that it was not thrown into the common pit for criminals. It was taken down and conveyed to a rock tomb, the family property of a sympathetic councillor, where it was provisionally secreted, as sundown had brought on the Sabbath, for the duration of which all worldly transactions had to cease. At sunrise on the day after the Sabbath, the little band of faithful women returned to the tomb fittingly to embalm the corpse. The corpse was gone. There were only the cloths in which it had been wrapped, and an unknown youth in a white robe who told the mourners that the dead man had risen and would shortly show himself, alive, to his friends.

And so he did. He showed himself not only to the nucleus of twelve and to the steadfast women, but to as many as five hundred different persons, at various times and in a variety of places, according to eye-witnesses, some of whom gave written testimony of the wonder. In most cases they did not immediately recognise him; one of the disciples even had the courage of his scepticism and asked to see and feel the

The Resurrection

wounds made by the nails and the spear with which Jesus' side had been slashed to ascertain that life was extinct. But they all received abundant proof of his identity, and drank in his instructions for the future, until, forty days after his mortal agony, he finally disappeared from human ken in a mountain cloud.

The resurrection of Jesus changed everything. It showed that he in truth was the Messiah, who moreover had promised to come again when the time was ripe, as the disciples were to work for that ripening. The disciples who had hidden in panic and despondency arose, even as their Master had arisen from the dead, intoxicated, inspired with joy and a marvellously justified faith, and came forward, never to flinch again, with the Good News of redemption and the conquest of death. For the Master with his blood had purchased the liberation of mankind at once from human sins and cosmic annihilation; and it was for his accredited messengers to spread his holy word wherever there were ears to hear. They were happy men, strong men, indomitable ever after because of what they knew. Nothing could touch them, and nothing make them swerve. The leading twelve were these:

Simon, nicknamed Kepha or Peter, the Rock, a fisherman of Galilee, expressly appointed as his deputy by Jesus, perhaps because of his seniority, perhaps because of the very human weaknesses he displayed from time to time and which bespoke a great potential of empathy;

Andrew, his brother, of the same calling;

James and John, the sons of Zebedee, sometimes nicknamed the Sons of Thunder for their ebullience, also Galilean fishermen; John was the youngest in years of the original disciples and was thought to be Jesus' favourite among them;

Thomas, a carpenter who had worked with Jesus at this trade in Nazareth – he was the one who would not believe without physical evidence;

Philip, a friend of Peter and Andrew, like them from Bethsaida, near Nazareth, and a one-time pupil of Jesus' kinsman and immediate forerunner John the Baptist. Philip introduced to Jesus one Nathanael – 'An Israelite indeed, in whom is no guile', Jesus commented: for when Nathanael was called to meet the man from Nazareth he first of all growled, 'What good thing ever came out of Nazareth?'

Bartholomew – none other than that same Nathanael, who as soon as he had spoken to the Master face to face acknowledged him the promised king of Israel;

Simon of Cana, previously belonging to the anti-Roman sect of Zealots;

James 'the Less,' in distinction from the son of Zebedee of the same name; and his brother Jude or Thaddaeus (these two were either sons of Jesus' putative father, Joseph, or nephews of Joseph);

Matthew or Levi, formerly of the detested and religiously under-privileged caste of tax-gatherers;

Judas of Kerioth, the hapless betrayer without whom the Passion would not have been enacted, and who afterwards hanged himself; replaced by –

Matthias, the only one whom Jesus had not personally chosen: he was elected by the rest after Jesus' departure, to make up their number again to twelve.

They were not alone. All along there had been others, 'hidden' or part-time assistants to Jesus, who had not like the twelve given up everything to wander with him and do his errands of preaching, healing, exorcising: among them members of the High Court of Jerusalem and other relations of Jesus – friends, well-wishers, converts in every walk of life.

For every name mentioned in the Gospels – like Nikodemos, Nicanor, Cleophas, Lazarus, Simon of Cyrene, Joseph of Arimathea, and all the duplicated Johns, Judes, and Marys – unnamed people whom Jesus had given healing or illumination, hailing his entry or bewailing his passage to Golgotha, flit across the scene. For every person standing out from the throng, sometimes by one briefly characterising gesture – like the young man (believed by some authorities to be Mark) who fled naked, leaving his shirt behind – there were, now 'seventy', now 'one hundred and twenty', now 'a great multitude' of shadowy individuals, on some of whom focus would sharpen later on.

To all of these Jesus had made his resurrection manifest, instilling in them a tremendous urge to communicate their experience. The circle of believers – believers in Jesus the Christ and his teaching – spread with a new impetus: and each believer was another apostle.

These people called themselves the saints, being united in a fellowship sanctified by the belief that the Messiah, the Christ had been here. Their detractors dubbed them Christians.

2

The Messengers

Anyone who has ever lost a beloved person through death – especially violent death, untimely death, death aggravated by injustice, torture, and opprobrium – anybody who has mourned one whom he believed great and good and of importance to humanity at large – anyone with this experience must appreciate the feelings of the saints. Anybody who has ever dreamed in his sleep that it was all a mistake, that the beloved person is still alive, then to wake up to the bitterness of un-changed loss – anyone so teased by a wishful imagination must under-stand what it meant to the followers of Jesus to know for a fact that in his case the dream was true.

The impact of the resurrection was all the more powerful because of the disappointment which had preceded it – when he in whom they had trusted as the preternaturally endowed king of Israel had perished – beaten, mocked, and evidently helpless – and the movement which he had been leading collapsed by the same token. Ever since it was shown that on the contrary the crucifixion proved the turning point of victory, there has been speculation on the deed of Judas.

There have been those who held that Judas was merely impatient to force the Master's hand so as to show the world here, now, im-mediately, that he was the Messiah. There have been others – suggesting that Jesus himself ordered Judas to act as he did, so as to accomplish the prophecy of a blood sacrifice which it is clear was the one he, Jesus, had by then adopted – clear from the whole change of mood that came over him directly he had decided to go to Jerusalem. For Jesus' remark, at the Last Supper, 'One of you shall betray me,' and his equi-vocal answers to the disciples' anxious questions thereupon, could equally well have been a veiled instruction as a prophecy; and what might not Judas have murmured in Jesus' ear when giving him the 'Judas' kiss? The shock to the unhappy man when he realised Jesus was going to be executed made life unbearable to him, so that he killed himself without waiting to see what would come of it. By any other interpretation Judas' treachery and subsequent remorse do not really make sense: the former would make him out a very unlikely man for Jesus to have chosen to work with him, and the latter would contradict even that unlikely possibility.

However that might be, the Resurrection served the Messianic purpose as no armed revolt or wizardry would have done – not least because it bore out Jesus' fundamental teaching by placing victory, too, once and for all on the spiritual plane, in such a way that everyone could understand this. Thus martyrdom and immortality became directly linked, also removing the reward of virtue right away from earthly prosperity, so that it could no longer be asked: 'Why does misfortune befall me, who have done everything to be good?' The cross, an emblem of the utmost worldly failure, had become the emblem of the utmost – because eternal – success. The human predicament was forever solved, resolved in bliss.

The lives of the saints were now devoted to a twofold purpose: first, to propagate the Good News, and secondly, to follow in the Master's footsteps all the time. At first this was simple enough, in the sense of being clear-cut. Their propaganda consisted of the substance of the great Sermon on the Mount – which itself crystallised Jesus' practical theology – plus the eye-witness accounts of his ministry and passion. To keep it all fresh in their hearts and to keep themselves in spiritual trim, they meanwhile emulated his manner of living and celebrated their brotherhood in certain commemorative ceremonies. There were two to begin with: baptism and the love feast.

Baptism, which Jesus had undergone at the hands of his elder cousin John, signified rebirth in the purified faith and simultaneously purification from sin through repentance. The communal meal, re-enacting the Lord's supper on the eve of his martyrdom, affirmed the union of the faithful with him and with one another. As for living up to his precepts, these were perfectly unambiguous: abandon private property, share what you are given for your labours with your fellows, and inculcate 'to all the world' the spiritual regeneration through unconditional faith and selfless love.

Once upon a time the children of Israel had been nomads. Although long since settled on the land, wandering was in their blood. The stimulus was constantly revived by the nature of their land – hilly, with wild, arid stretches between scattered communities – as well as by the wider dispersal of their co-religionists. (At the Pentecostal descent of the Holy Ghost upon the saints of Jerusalem, they were heard to speak in the tongues of the following nationals assembled for the festival: 'Parthians, and Medes, and Elamites, and dwellers in Mesopotamia, Judaea, Cappadocia, Pontus, Asia, Phrygia and Pamphylia, Egypt and Libya, Rome, Crete and Arabia,' to which might have been added Gaul, Spain, Germany, and the mainland and islands of Greece.) The inhabitants of Palestine thought nothing of traversing the country backwards and forwards on foot. Jesus' mother had made the ninety-mile journey to Bethlehem when pregnant; the only time when Jesus rode instead of walking was in fulfilment of the prophecy that the Anointed would enter Jerusalem on an ass. There was incessant traffic to and from Jerusalem, branching in all directions of the Diaspora. News was fairly regular and punctual; communications, considering the very primitive channels and frequent dangers on the way, were

St Luke painting the Madonna

surprisingly efficient. The saints soon lodged their tale in many places, forming as many germ-cells of 'Christian' groups within the body of 'Torah' (Law) Jewry.

Luke's description of a mass conversion ('about three thousand souls' in one haul) in the Acts of the Apostles gives a palpable account of the alluring, serene harmony which suffused such groups: 'And all that believed were together and had all things in common . . . and sold their possessions and goods, and parted them to all men, as every man had need. And they, continuing daily with one accord in worship and breaking bread from house to house, did eat their meat with gladness and singleness of heart, praising God, and having favour with all the people . . . And with great power gave the apostles witness of the resurrection of the Lord Jesus: and great grace was upon them all.'

Once again the Jewish Establishment had reason to be perturbed and took the ringleaders of the indomitable movement into custody for examination. 'Now when they [the Council] saw the boldness of Peter and John, and perceived that they were unlearned and ignorant men, they marvelled.' Jesus, himself a scholar though also practising a manual craft as was the custom, evidently had known what he was doing when selecting those forthright fisherfolk to be his spokesmen. Judging by the effect, to hear them was to credit their story: it must have seemed they had not got it in them to fabricate such things. For at this stage, that is *after* the resurrection, even the top men of the ecclesiastical hierarchy were so nonplussed by the adamant confidence of Peter and John that, 'marvelling', they let the pair off with a warning.

The Jews took the second commandment very seriously and eschewed portraiture. No images of either Jesus or his saints were made till something like three centuries after his death. Thus it is to artists of much later times that we owe a very misleading general impression of the principals. For well over a thousand years none of them was ever shown without a halo or other unmistakable indications of exceptional quality, promoting the unconscious inference that this was what they looked like in life. But they did not have halos when they lived, nor were they clad in glory. They were poor men who tramped the country-side. For all that Jesus counted his descent from King David, for all that Matthew was by birth a Levite member of the hereditary priesthood, there was nothing to tell, by looking at them, that they were *not* lawless blasphemers; and is not eloquence reckoned the mark of the demagogue, death the time-honoured wages of heresy?

Similarly John, 'the disciple whom the Lord loved' according to the Gospel that bears his name, came to be envisaged as a gentle, almost feminine creature – most ill-suited to Jesus' epithet for John and his brother, 'the Sons of Thunder'. ('Shall we ask the Lord to bring down fire from heaven to consume them?' John and James eagerly asked Jesus when a Samaritan village had denied him hospitality.) Peter – usually depicted as already elderly at the Last Supper, though still hale and hearty thirty years hence – was impulsive rather than choleric; but the meek stance which in the distant future would become associated with saintliness would scarcely have served him or any of his fellow-evangelists at the time. They had to be hardy, forceful, even aggressive in their enthusiasm, to make it so catching.

But they could not be everywhere at once, those who had known Jesus in the flesh or during the forty days after the crucifixion. There were hundreds of people who had anecdotes about him or remembered passages from his speeches and conversations; presently there were thousands more to pass them on at second hand. Different versions complemented each other; for the People of the Book it was the obvious course to write them down, for secure transmission.

These jottings, made by men who though literate were 'unlearned and ignorant' for the most part, were not initially conceived as lasting documents. They were notes, memoranda, for current use. The second coming of the Messiah was expected, if not hourly, almost any day: hence the hurry. For themselves, the saints looked forward to the Day of Judgment with ardent longing – but there were millions of mankind yet to be saved. It was only when it began to be realised that the day might be much farther off than the faithful had assumed – that they themselves might never even live to see it – that the need for a proper record became at all acute. Old men forget; for that matter, this first crop of saints might not all live to grow very old.

The attitude of the orthodox authorities towards the Christian sect fast began to harden again, as the infection of anti-legalism, heretic eschatology, and primitive communism spread – so it must have seemed to the conservative – like a plague. What with the theocratic pattern of Jewish society as a whole, the sect appeared to carry the threat not only of anarchy, but of provoking the Almighty to turning against Israel for good. Soon it would become necessary to set down what happened to the apostles themselves, over and above what they had to tell about Jesus, as they were being persecuted in their own right.

Jesus had transacted all his ministry by word of mouth. He had said many things, on different occasions, in different places and in different moods, and adapted to different audiences. But now his every word was precious, not to be lost, but rather to be treated (for general application) *as* a divine utterance – whether uttered in a set context, or jokingly, or from some momentary irritation. Fixed in writing, there were no distinctions of tone; all the sayings of Jesus were equal, in weight and sacrosanctity. The saints now set about collecting and preserving them, more seriously, as the Christian congregations of Judaea perforce went underground.

So far the apostles, always geared to missionary activity, had concentrated wholly on preaching the resurrection and the doctrine of the Christ, conferring the baptismal sacrament of penitence on proselytes and organising the resulting cells around the love feast. With the constant growth of the movement administrative problems were raised which required the appointment of officials to regulate them satisfactorily. Thus the first seven deacons were instituted in the Christian congregation of Jerusalem, following a proposal by the Twelve which was democratically adopted.

The issue of administration had come to a head over a complaint by the Greek-speaking membership against those who spoke Hebrew – or rather Aramaic, Hebrew being mostly relegated to liturgical purposes. Israel had for some time past been divided between diehard traditionalists and liberals, the former clinging to the fear of pagan contamination and refusing to have anything to do with any aspect of non-Jewish culture, and the latter pursuing mutual assimilation, with the promise of God to Abraham, '*All* the races of the world shall find a blessing through thy posterity', for their slogan. Greek was the *lingua franca* of the Mediterranean world and all its outposts under the eagles of Rome, and hellenic culture was a universal index of education.

The first seven deacons were all of the order of hellenised Jews

St Stephen, the first martyr

(at least, six of them were: Stephen, Philip, Prochorus, Nicanor, Timon, Parmenas – the seventh, Nicolas, was actually a Greek convert to Judaism). Especially blessed by the Twelve and thus 'consecrated' in positions of authority, these men brought a new ingredient to the Christian synthesis. They were younger, more educated, less hide-bound than the Old Guard of worthies from the Galilean countryside, and fanned a spirit of fresh enterprise.

The most enterprising of them, Stephen, was the first saint to become a martyr. Peter's policy of simple proselytising – 'Feed my sheep!' within the same old grazing grounds – was not enough for Stephen. He, rather, took his cue from another word of the Master, 'One does not put new wine into old bottles, else the bottles burst and the wine runs out; put new wine into new bottles, and both will be preserved.' The old enclosures must be broken down, new pastures opened up, for the sheep to flourish; the new wine of Christian doctrine would never be accommodated in the old, law-bound container but called for a completely new form. Where Peter merely advocated Jesus, Stephen indicted and assailed the citadel of orthodoxy in its entire structure.

Arraigned for trial, Stephen so far from defending himself poured forth an impassioned précis of the whole of Israel's religious history

Heralding the birth of the Messiah: the Annunciation, showing the
Archangel Gabriel and the Virgin Mary with the figure of God the Father
in the background.

The Nativity, a painting of the great east window of the Church of St Peter Mancroft, Norwich, showing shepherds serenading the Child: a late representation, though medieval in spirit. Note the human touch of the midwife warming the baby's night-gown.

A third-century sarcophagus depicting Christ as the Good Shepherd, the most common image of Christ in the early Church, which at first fought shy of depicting him at all. The beard which subse-quently came to be regarded as typical has not yet appeared; the youthful shepherd is a clean-shaven Roman, not a hirsute Hebrew.

The Almighty Creator seen in
the image of man: 'God the
Father seated in Majesty',
drawing by Pietro Perugino
(c. 1446–1524).

External ritual and gesture:
the infant Jesus initiated into
the Jewish religious community. 'Circumcision', sketch
by Raffaellino del Garbo
(c. 1466–1524).

The Baptism of Christ, a fifth-century mosaic from the centre of the dome in the Baptistry of the Orthodox at Ravenna. The Holy Spirit descends in the form of a dove; the river is represented by the figure of a god, in accordance with hellenistic tradition. The beard, a compromise between the unclipped hair of orthodox Jewry and the bare, classical face, has now evolved.

in proof of his accusations against the prevailing system. He was howled down and dragged off to summary execution (governor Pilate was away, himself to answer charges in Rome). The traditional Jewish punishment for blasphemy was death by stoning: an early method of distributing the blood-guilt of the executioner, as no one in a crowd of good citizens hurling the stones would ever know who had finally despatched the delinquent.

The manner of Stephen's death made a great impression. He knelt down without attempting to shield himself from the stones, loudly calling on Jesus to receive his soul and not to hold their sin against his murderers. 'And when he had said this, he fell asleep . . . And devout men carried Stephen to his burial and made great lamentation over him.'

But it was the signal for systematic persecution in the capital of Jewry. The saints henceforth had to hold their assemblies in secret and at night, with cryptic passwords and code signs becoming added to their ritual vocabulary. The hellenists among them, too easily identified with Stephen, left the city for their divers home towns and countries. In this way the first effective step was taken to build up Christian synagogues abroad, 'yea, even to the ends of the earth', just as Jesus had bidden.

The rest had to stay, and endure. One hellenised Jew stayed on also, in the opposite camp, however. He was 'a young man named Saul', who had come to Jerusalem to study under the most celebrated Jewish sage and scholar of the day, Rabbi Gamaliel. Saul came from the Greek town of Tarsus in Cilicia, where his family plied a highly respectable trade and held Roman citizenship. He thus was rather a cut above most of the Christian rank and file; speaking both Greek and Latin, studious and cultivated, with a strong theological vocation, and orthodox to the bone.

Saul was a spectator at the execution of Stephen and looked after the clothes of the men who took part in the killing. On him Stephen's heroic stand had the effect of strengthening his antipathy to the Christian sect – seeing that it bred such heedless fanatics. Or so it then appeared to him; possibly Stephen's special pleading of Judaic history had got under his skin, in more than one discomforting way.

Saul placed himself at the disposal of the Jerusalem authorities, to help exterminate the heresy.

3
The Authors

All the Western world knows about the subsequent history of that young man under his Roman name of Paulus. Of all the builders of the new, universal religion he became the master architect. If Jesus was at once the foundation and the keystone, Paul laid down the ground plan of the foursquare edifice. To Jesus the Son of God, Paul was the theologian.

A lasting system such as Paul's was not wrought in a day. It took him over thirty years – a small outlay of time, when all is said, for twenty centuries' return, to date, and of course the merest nothing in terms of eternity. In point of human energy, he invested everything he had.

It had really started long before the famous, blinding day on the Damascus road, if a Talmudic reference is to be trusted concerning the trouble Rabbi Gamaliel had had with 'that pupil's impudence in matters of learning'. Certain hints by Paul himself corroborate that he had suffered for some time from secret doubts, and the abrupt wholeheartedness with which he threw himself into the service of the cause he had been so vigorously combating smacks of relief. If, steeped in the Law and loth to write off his relevant accomplishments to start all over again from scratch, he had been secretly worrying whether a path depending on the human will were not too easy to lead to the goal of salvation – this would explain both his defensive fury against the Christians and his conversion without benefit of any external human influence. It might even be significant that, having listened to Stephen's revolutionary diatribe and joined in the clamour for Stephen's blood, Paul yet held back from the actual execution, standing guard over the executioners' clothes being his excuse. 'It is hard for thee to kick against the pricks' – the pricks of a nagging intellectual conscience – The Voice said to him understandingly before Damascus.

Paul is the only outstanding figure among the early saints of whom

The conversion of St Paul

we have a physical description: short, bandy-legged, bald, with heavy eyebrows meeting between his eyes, and a hooked nose. Yet it was said of him that sometimes he looked more like an angel than a man. The bandy legs, in the son of a distinguished, well-to-do family, whose infant diet can scarcely have been deficient, in an environment where there was anything but shortage of sun, suggest some congenital handicap. The fact that his steady travelling companion on his apostolic wanderings was Luke, a physician, might be fortuitous – but then, it might not. The 'angelic' look would only be perceived in animation, when the force of his emotional vitality would shine and crackle about the little man – not the sort of thing to go down in a passport, like the listed physical details. For it is thought that these came from a sort of credential such as the first missionaries carried for identification in places where they were not known: a very necessary precaution, since before long the Christian communities were to be haunted by *agents provocateurs*.

The description of Paul is in an 'apocryphal' text. But 'apocryphal', in connection with the Bible, merely means that the texts so defined were not included in a specific, authorised canon. Authorised by whom? By men, and men living long after the events recorded. Though it might be unfair to call such selections arbitrary, opportunist would not be too reckless an adjective. Until the Renaissance there was no such thing as critical analysis of texts. A given canon would be put together on the basis of what was most suitable to the underlying didactic purpose.

Paul, when he first started studying the depositions of the saints who had known Jesus personally, had not a few to choose from. By the time the Four Gospels we know came to be written, there were a good many more. The ones of Matthew, Mark, and Luke are commonly dated AD 50–63, that of John towards the end of the first century, and Luke's Book of Acts about the mid-sixties. Paul's own epistles were written between AD 49 and 66 or 67, the year of his death. So Mark, Luke, and John, in all probability, already had Paul's theology to go by for orientation of their biographies of the Lord. Mark and Luke were in close daily contact with Paul for many years, and their compositions certainly would have been submitted to both Paul and Peter – Mark moreover being Peter's aide-de-camp, interpreter, and secretary. And Peter had then come a long way from Galilee, in every sense, and was sharing the leadership with Paul, to put it mildly. For it very much looks as if by then Paul was the real leader, using the venerated name of Peter as a front. Paul had frequently to re-persuade Peter to his, Paul's, non-restrictive policy, and prod him to speak out for it.

Only Matthew wrote in Aramaic and primarily for Jews of Jewish birth. The other three wrote in Greek for a wider public, and Luke of course was himself a Gentile Greek by origin, and so willy-nilly addressed himself most of all to converts of his own kind. Luke like Paul was a born writer, where the other three took up the stylus on demand of exigency – John, the last to do so, in extreme old age: at the very least he must have been approaching ninety.

Matthew was careful to provide comprehensive coverage, in orderly progression complete with historical data.

Mark was anxious to commit to posterity everything that Peter, the chief apostle, remembered of Jesus, without troubling too much about chronological sequence or internal cohesion – to get it written was the important thing. He also tried as he went along to explain

St John the Evangelist

whatever points his audience (he wrote in Rome) might not understand; for instance he incorporated bits of information concerning traditional Jewish ritual and added that the Jordan is a river.

Luke was an artist: as well as practising medicine he also painted. His governing interest as a writer was neither theological nor circumstantial: it was to make the story and personality of Jesus as real and compelling as he could. Luke concentrated on the human element.

And John – John had come an even longer way than Peter. He outlived Peter by thirty years, and only then began to write – when there was nothing else for him to do on the relatively desert isle of Patmos to where he had been deported by the Emperor Domitian. John the angry young 'Son of Thunder' had mellowed, or – if one thinks of his Book of Revelation – at all events had learnt to sublimate and spiritualise his militancy. John had witnessed a massed crescendo of persecutions of Christians in the Empire, to which the terror under Nero that saw the end of Peter and Paul was but a ragged prelude. He had had a full six decades of entirely religious occupation, with half of that period to mull over the Gospel experience all by himself as he was the sole survivor from the time of Jesus' ministry. When he had first left Palestine John the simple fisherman was still young enough to become influenced by the trends of Greek philosophy then springing all round; the would-be hurler of fire and brimstone matured into the first Christian mystic. The task to which he gave the last years of his long life was to round off through the vehicle of his personal memoirs the message of invulnerable spiritual sovereignty. So what John wrote was designedly a supplement to the other narratives, lifting the incidents of the plot into the sphere of metaphysical symbolism. Even as Paul emerged the founder of Christian theology, John in his old age became the founder of Christian philosophy. As Paul explicated and amplified the Christian principles, so John encompassed that ultimate reconciliation of material disaster with spiritual triumph of which the cross was the emblem.

All this is taking the canon as it stands, without possible reservations as to genuineness of authorship or the accuracy of copyists' transcriptions – just as for the present purpose the Gospel story itself is taken as it stands, without speculative alternatives.

If there were errors, omissions or misunderstandings, if distortions occurred in the interests of propaganda – that would still be irrelevant to a study of developments which took place *on the basis* of such flaws.

Certainly the Community of Saints, later known as the Church, took infinite care according to its then lights in establishing the authenticity of the writings which were to be officially adopted and rejecting those which appeared fanciful and impossible to substantiate – among them innumerable embroideries on those tracts of Jesus' life that had remained obscure to the disciples, and all such biographies of the whole cast of characters involved in the drama of the Passion which similarly prompted a suspicion of imaginative treatment. To be sure, the literature condemned as apocryphal did not thereby lose its audience and disappear: indeed, many a heresy was to stem from it in times to come. For the Community of Saints, like all human institutions, was composed of partial, fallible humans, and like all institutions evolved vested interests which in turn would decry dissident opinion as heretical.

Jesus had freed the living spirit of the faith from the prison of the Law whose accretions had petrified around it. Christianity as it was shaped by Paul and John, co-ordinated by Peter, and disseminated by the saints at large, was essentially a missionary briefing for ideological shock troops. It was a dynamic method – naturally, as it looked forward to the day of the Messiah's second advent. It was not a futuristic blueprint for a time when the Messiah was actually reigning: the kingdom of God would take care of itself. The saints had no conception of a Church victorious on earth without a corollary end of the present world. They made no plans for that.

4

The Organizers

After the killing of Stephen (c. AD 32), most of the hellenist saints, then, retreated to the Jewish colonies in Greek territories, where advance news of the Christian revelation had generally preceded them, and where the orthodox synagogues proved on the whole remarkably receptive to their teaching. Conditioned to be more flexible and open to outside influences, in cultural give-and-take with their pagan environment, the religious authorities of these enclaves did not have the automatic intransigence of the supreme hierarchy at Jerusalem, and, even though acknowledging that hierarchy, were not necessarily swayed by its example in matters like this. Oddly enough, the stereotype legalism which Jesus sought to break had had the effect of leaving Jewry more tolerant of doctrinal innovations than of departures from ritual tradition.

Outside Palestine, the first clashes between the harbingers of the new and the custodian of the old occurred, not over the fundamental question of whether Jesus was the Christ, but over violations of ritual purity and ritual xenophobia. Hellenised Jews might admit much that was salubrious in Greek secular civilisation, but still drew the line at eating unclean – that is, forbidden – food, or food contaminated by proximity to ritually unclean matter, in the houses of their Gentile neighbours; and so on.

This principle also led to the first difficulties among the saints in Palestine – over and above their difficulties with the orthodox. As well as falling foul of the Jewish Council, Peter was attacked by his own flock for consorting with uncircumcised filth-eaters in the cause of evangelism. On top of tending and extending the Christian underground the senior apostle had to defend his onerous position from internal hostility. Those of the Twelve and their lieutenants who pushed forward into other parts of the country – Samaria, Syria, Phoenicia – as Jesus had bidden the disciples, came up against the same thing.

And this was not just wilful contentiousness on the part of their critics. As well as directing the faithful to baptise and instruct all the nations of the earth, Jesus at another juncture had also proclaimed that he wished to perfect, not to set aside, the Law and the Prophets; from which many of his saints drew the inference that they must be more rather than less strict in observance than other Jews. Happily an impasse was averted by a vision vouchsafed to Peter in which the Lord definitively rescinded the food prohibitions and with them the exclusiveness which would have rendered world-wide missions a contradiction in terms. Even so, the old habits died hard, and presently fresh points of debate were raised, still to do with outward forms: should the Christian Sabbath still be celebrated on the same day as the orthodox? Seeing that the orthodox fasted on Mondays and Thursdays, ought not Christians to do it on Wednesdays and Fridays?

Without the fusing fires of persecution, it is possible that the sect might have succumbed to multiple fission. But as the sect had grown, so had persecution accelerated, and it became still more heated upon the accession of a new king in Judaea. Herod Agrippa, scion of the Edomite Herodian dynasty, satellite of Rome, and a reformed rake, in guilty consciousness of his non-Jewish blood set out to prove himself irreproachably stern in Jewish puritan zeal. In the short, sharp reign of Herod Agrippa the community of saints was harried more and more severely by police and informers. Among the victims was James the brother of John, the first of the Twelve to be martyred. Peter, who was taken in the same wave of arrests once more got away, but only by a miracle.

Peter now 'went elsewhere', most probably to Antioch. In this Syrian city, one of the richest and most important in the whole Roman Empire, there was a large and prosperous Jewish settlement, of the hellenised kind. Here the comrades of Stephen had worked with notable success, so that there had developed a sizeable Christian minority not only of native Jews but also of native pagans. The problem which so agitated the saints of Judaea had apparently solved itself naturally at Antioch: accustomed to close neighbourly co-operation, Jewish and Gentile Christians had grown together fully integrated and shared their love feasts as a matter of course.

One of the leading Pentecostal recruits to the apostolic band, one Joseph renamed Barnabas, a Cypriot Levite distinguished for his

The beheading of St James

charity and goodwill, had already been despatched to appraise the situation in Antioch, and he reported with enthusiasm on Christian solidarity and expansion there. (It was here, too, that the Greek form of the sect's Messianic sobriquet – the actual word, Christian – first came to be honoured by serious usage.)

With the Herodian terror, followed by the presumed sojourn of Peter at Antioch, the centre of gravity of the Christian movement shifted to that city. The demand for assistant teachers and administrators was insatiable, and Saul-Paul after his dramatic conversion served his evangelical apprenticeship under Joseph-Barnabas at Antioch.

The practice of name-changing had an ancient tradition behind it. It is a common feature of primitive societies that the adult acquires his proper name upon crossing the threshold of maturity and full initiation into the tribe, the infant's name being but a temporary convenience; often, too, the adult name carries a significant, portentous reference. Jewish myth was rich in instances of symbolic changes of name: the nomad patriarch Abram ('the Father is exalted') became Abraham ('the father of many nations') when Isaac was born to him. Jacob the heir of Isaac became Israel ('god-fighter') after he had wrestled with the angel. By-names like Peter or Barnabas (rendered as either 'son of consolation' or 'son of exhortation') were useful among a people with a comparatively small fund of tribal given-names, but at the same time formed a testimonial of the bearer's role under Christ.

Paul had a second name ready-made as a Roman citizen with obligatory Latin sponsorship and nomenclature. He only needed to give up 'Saul the Benjaminite' to proclaim the Christian-universal outlook he imbibed at Antioch and mark his spiritual rebirth. 'Paul of Tarsus', excellent outside Hebrew territory, was however no recommendation in Jerusalem. On his next visit, where he had last been seen as a mortal enemy of the Christian sect, the saints not unnaturally met him with mistrust and aversion which Peter and Barnabas, who came with him, had hard work to overcome.

Though these highly respected two vouched for him and the extraordinary capabilities which they had watched him unfolding at Antioch and elsewhere, the Jerusalem saints could never quite forget that Paul alone was an entirely self-made apostle. He had never known Jesus in life, nor had he been co-opted by the Lord's disciples as Matthias, Barnabas, Mark, Stephen and the other deacons had been. Where everybody else to whom the resurrected Master had appeared could produce witnesses corroborating this, Paul's visions had been seen by no one but himself (though admittedly the Lord had announced Saul's conversion to a Damascene disciple). But Paul was already becoming known specifically as the apostle to the Gentiles; and the Galilean old guard were no match for one of Paul's intellect and dominating character; the movement could not do without him now – even had he had the least intention to let it ride without him. So long as Paul managed to keep Peter on his side, he would prevail. The Lord assisted Paul in securing Peter's backing.

Jerusalem was played out as an apostolic headquarters, save in nostalgic loyalty. At source, Jewish particularism continued going strong among the Christians there who clung tenaciously to the old taboos and shibboleths which were an obsolete dead-weight upon the progress of the faith abroad. Before long, the leadership saw no other way but to prohibit the prohibitions, outright, instead of allowing observance to be optional as heretofore. Barnabas went so far as to declare the Jewish customs incompatible with perfect faith; Paul declared pure faith the one and only religious prerequisite: 'Anybody who believes in Jesus Christ is a Jew.' And Peter stopped vacillating and endorsed the ruling.

With that, and with the eventual destruction (AD 70) of the Jewish national state after its last abortive insurrection against Rome, Christianity finally became emancipated from its homeland. Rome took over the entire governance of Judaea, the fostering of Christianity, and the parallel attempt to stamp it out.

What was it made the Christian appeal so potent and at the same time attracted the consistent hostility of the secular authorities even where they had no theocratic axe to grind? On both counts, the root of the answer lay in the conquest of death.

The attractions of Christianity corresponded to three basic factors unique to the human species: the foreknowledge of death, the urge to understand, and the need of articulate communication beyond bare biological signalling. Christianity provided a satisfactory explanation of the scheme of things that left no more loopholes and discrepancies, with a story line tracing a cogent pattern from the Creation through the Fall to the Redemption; it rendered death not the end but rather the true beginning of individual life; and it provided a subject of constant, higher communication. It made earthly life worth living even at its most wretched and added an extra dimension to it even at its best. Man's primordial bugbear, Fear itself, was slain: there was nothing left to be afraid of, under God. The gap between virtue and reward was closed, as virtue had its reward guaranteed in heaven, where there resided the only true reality. The void of infinity was filled, with meaning. Man the seeker after transcendental anchorage had come home.

If the material world did not matter and life did not really begin till after death, all earthly disabilities were abolished. If salvation was by faith alone, salvation was in everybody's reach: slaves, cripples,

females, persons tainted by unsavoury occupations – all could attain
to the full human status so far denied them by other systems. All men
were brothers, potentially equal inheritors of the Covenant, every
living soul equally precious to God: a prospect filling the believer with
a marvellous sense of purpose and optimism, which it was positively
incumbent upon him to pass on.

But unbelievers saw the reverse side of the medal. If earthly disabilities were abolished, so surely would be earthly obligations. If
social categories were nullified, what became of the class structure?
If fear and material well-being were of no account, what became of
earthly incentives and deterrents? If private property were to be
abnegated, nobody and nothing would be safe: bereft of substance,
all law and order must collapse. So, by the sort of irony that history
is full of, the 'pie in the sky' message, for which Christianity has in
our day been denounced as an insidious tranquilliser, was regarded
when it was new as dangerously inflammatory.

In vain Christians protested that their Master had not preached
revolt and anarchy but on the contrary absolute submissiveness to
secular authority: 'My kingdom is not of this world' – that so far from
licensing aggression in any form he had forbidden even retaliation
against violence and prescribed not merely sufferance but love of one's
enemies.

Maybe so; but meanwhile their very pacifism could be construed as
a menace to an Empire which was dependent on its military to hold it
together. The earliest recorded Roman converts to Christ had both
been centurions of the legions stationed in Palestine – members of the
armed forces and officers to boot. Furthermore, their vaunted peaceable
intentions notwithstanding, the Christians were causing civil unrest
wherever they set foot. Uproar and rioting marked their trail from one
Jewish community of the Empire to another; and even where, in Greece
and Asia Minor, they had virtually taken over local synagogues, the
next thing was internecine bickering and factional rivalry. At Ephesus,
the Empire's gateway to the East, very serious disturbances broke out
as the Christians offended the religious sensibilities of their pagan
neighbours: threatening as they did the supremacy of the goddess
Artemis of the Ephesians, who was a famous tourist draw and whose
cult constituted a major local industry.

The imperial central government ruled that, being disowned by the recognised Jewish authorities, the Christian sect had no legal existence: which made Christian persistence a civil misdemeanour.

The one styled the Apostle to the Gentiles, Paul, was frequently found at the storm centres in those early days. Although disclaiming particular rhetorical ability, Paul clearly was an exceedingly gifted evangelist cum organizer. (The only occasion on record when he failed to impress was at Athens, where his story of the dead man walking among his friends for forty days raised gales of homeric laughter. On the other hand, at Lystra his effect was such that the populace acclaimed him as an incarnation of the god Mercury and tried to drag him off to 'his' altar to be worshipped.)

More than his colleagues, Paul was concerned with the future of Christianity rather than evocation of the sublime past of Jesus' ministry and passion. His travels all over the eastern Mediterranean seaboard, the Taurus mountains and desert tracts inland – braving cockleshell navigation and climatic extremes – which added up to something like seven thousand miles in thirteen years – gives an indication of his driving force and stamina. One is also tempted to see herein evidence of an initially poor physique, responding as so often to the spur of the seemingly impossible. Paul survived flogging, imprisonment and stoning – when though left for dead he rose with his wounds miraculously made whole: whole, that is, except for the permanent sores on his brow, his hands, his feet, and his side, which stayed with him for life – the first, modest example of the stigmata.

Everywhere he went Paul left behind him well-knit communities of saints, adapted to optimal function in their respective environments. But as he moved on, the provincial leaders did not always remain sure of their ground, nor did they always feel certain how to solve unforeseen problems arising afterwards.

Thus what was probably the most far-reaching correspondence in the whole of history came into being. For the most part patiently, only sometimes with ill-suppressed exasperation, the overworked apostle reiterated his instructions – also answering preliminary enquiries from communities he had yet to visit – in a series of letters which in course of time were taken as enshrining the nuclear whole of Christian theology and institutions, for ever after. As Jesus was the interpreter of godhead, Paul became the interpreter of Jesus: but then there followed generation upon generation of interpreters of Paul.

Returning once more to Jerusalem in the year 58 to report on his missions, Paul walked straight into the arms of his one-time friends but now bitterest enemies, the Jewish traditionalists who regarded him as a traitor by defection to Christianity. He was set upon by an enraged mob, rescued by the Roman guard, and taken off for a summary beating, whereupon he asserted his Roman citizenship and eventually demanded his statutory right to a trial in Rome. After many delays and vicissitudes he got his desired transportation, and set foot for the first time on Italian soil, in the spring of AD 60, under official imperial auspices and with a sympathetic military escort.

Pending his trial (which hung fire another two years) he was allowed to lodge in a rented house, and immediately became the hub of the already numerous Christian community in the capital of the Empire.

5

The Golden Age

In centuries to come the formative, precarious phases of Christianity were to be looked back on with an ever-growing nostalgia. The idyllic perfection of Eden before the Fall, which served as a conventional template for the Millennium, was modified so as to embrace the period of sainthood under conditions of perpetual emergency: thus having the bland atmosphere of everlasting peace braced with the high-toned tension of war. In retrospect the first three hundred years were to appear as an age of innocence, when the issues were stark and plain, with everybody knowing exactly what to do, everybody loving one another, sharing dangers, aims and all things else in a complete unanimity which was also blessedly constructive.

For the Primitive Church did not just cower in the catacombs: it built the catacombs in the first place, for one thing. The catacombs formed the compound necropolis of the Christian community in Rome, and they convey an idea of its continuous growth.

Inhumation was a Jewish not a Roman funerary custom, but Roman law was tolerant of alien rites *qua* rites and respectful of the dead. All land in which the dead were laid to rest, whether in form of ashes or bodies, was held absolutely sacred; that it must lie outside the city walls was the only stipulation. Funeral clubs and collective tombs for the poor were encouraged, and even when the Christian religion was no longer merely unrecognised but actually outlawed, nobody stopped its hunted devotees from properly interring their deceased. From first to last the Christian cemeteries were laid out openly, openly frequented, and never desecrated, even at the worst. But even at the best of times – that is up to AD 64, before the great fire of Rome ushered in the long era of most virulent persecution – it took courage to buy the necessary land and march about in funeral processions, thus publicly declaring affiliation to a creed which was not considered respectable.

'Such a nice chap: what a pity he's a Christian!' 'So intelligent: how

Six of Christ's miracles. From left to right: the Feeding of the
Five Thousand, the Raising of Lazarus, the Healing of the Blind Man,
the Wedding at Cana, the Healing of the Paralytic, the Healing
of the Leper. From the Andrews diptych in the Victoria and
Albert Museum.

The Last Supper, sixth-century mosaic from the church of St Apollinaris, Ravenna, with the curious feature of fish on the table, recalling the miracle of the Five Thousand.

'Deposition', thirteenth-century polychrome wood-carving at the Cathedral of Volterra, showing the sorrowing Mother, Joseph of Arimathaea, a soldier extracting a nail from Christ's foot, and John the Beloved Disciple.

The Resurrection and Ascension, ivory panel, c. 400. The garden is indicated by the tree on the left, with the soldiers asleep by the sepulchre beneath. At the bottom of the panel the angel is seen announcing the Resurrection to the three Marys, and above them Christ in the presence of the Apostles ascends to glory by the Father's helping hand.

A twelfth-century mosaic from the Cathedral of Torcello near Venice. At the top Christ is shown in Limbo, in the centre he presides over the resurrection of the dead on the Day of Judgement, and in the lower portion the blessed are separated from the damned.

could he have himself converted to Christianity?' These are among
the remarks recorded by Tertullian around the end of the first century,
along with the gay anecdote about the Roman cuckold whose wife
suddenly began to tread the path of virtue. The husband asked her
why, and, learning that she had turned Christian, implored her to
resume her adulterous courses rather than inflict on him this worse
disgrace.

Although, then, educated, well-to-do, and even patrician Romans
were joining the outlandish sect, it continued for some time to be
identified with foreigners and low-class riff-raff. The city of Rome was
full of Barbarians of every description, costume and complexion,
representing the whole human spectrum of the Empire's provinces;
the native Latin population at that time was physically a minority,
and the number of the free-born, let alone ruling section was propor-
tionately small. The Gospel, addressed in the first instance to the poor
and laden, and accordingly propagated in the first instance mainly by
such people, invariably made its first impact on their kind – on folk
to whom the doctrine of metaphysical freedom, consolation and eternal
recompense had most to offer. Slaves, small shopkeepers, artisans,
fundamentally despised and fundamentally homesick provincials,
generally responded to the message first. Not the least part of its per-
suasive power was the effect it wrought upon those who now relayed
it, the liberation and serenity which palpably informed their spirit.
Time and again lightning conversions occurred, without the aid of
miracles; time and again – yet not with quite such regularity as to
prompt an automatic cynicism – there were accounts of informers,
magistrates, jailers, executioners won over by the example of Christian
fortitude in adversity. With good reason were the early martyrs able
to feel that their blood was a precious fertiliser as well as sanctifying
themselves in imitation of Christ.

The Christian was also beset with less heroic tribulations. While
he was not restricted in his intercourse with pagans by the stringent
anti-contamination rubric of Judaism proper, still the demands of
spiritual hygiene raised a host of difficulties every day. The residual
prohibitions of Christianity all hinged directly on essentially pagan practices, like partaking of blood, or the flesh of animals sacrificed to pagan
gods, and including magic and sexual irregularities. But this also meant

From the *Ars Moriendi*: Good Inspiration against Despair

that the Christian might not take oath on pagan deities – which was the legal mode of contract: so how was a Christian merchant to carry on in business? The Christian might not set his hand to fashioning heathen idols: so how were shoals of Christian craftsmen now to make a living? A Christian pedagogue must not teach classical mythology, which was the framework of Roman education; a Christian judge must not pass sentence involving bloodshed, which more or less encompassed the whole scale of criminal punishments. Christians might not participate in heathen festivals, of which there were many, nor in the favourite blood sports of the circus. If they wished to be Christians, brothel-keepers, playwrights, actors, gladiators, astrologers, soothsayers and so forth had to change their professions. Upright pagan fathers disinherited their wayward Christian sons; husbands less meek than the one cited by Tertullian disowned Christian wives – whether or not the Christian wives in question would consider themselves divorced.

For this was another innovation of Christianity. Marriage was declared indissoluble save by death or 'unchastity' meaning a union in the forbidden degree of kinship (fornication and adultery were held sinful but not legally punishable, since Jesus had himself granted forgiveness for such transgressions, contingent upon due repentance). The abolition of divorce was a great boon to women, hitherto virtually unprotected against marital vagary by any Law, Jewish or Gentile. Motherhood also derived a bonus from the uncompromising prohibition of bloodshed, as in all pagan societies it was lawful to expose newborn infants at the discretion of the head of the house, which – with exceptions proving the rule – caused much heartbreak.

Still there were enough hardships attached to the new faith to put off as many people as were attracted by the challenge of its discipline and its deferred promise. There were also enough people on all levels of society to welcome the arrival of a group against whom everyone could inveigh to his heart's content, a kind of universal butt and scapegoat and safety valve. It was surely this which kept going the sadistic persecutions of so harmless a group, not only in the reigns of psychopathic monsters like Nero and Domitian but also under otherwise humane and balanced emperors like Vespasian, Titus, and the Antonines.

When Paul first came to Rome Nero, last of the Julio-Claudians, had been on the throne some six years and the *Pax Romana* which his predecessors had consolidated held fast. The motley capital might have its periodic moments of ferment, but the world-spanning network of roads radiating from it, the seas swept clean of pirates, the power of law and order throughout the Empire, were safe and sound. Without the efficiency and essential beneficence of the Roman administration Paul would have been lynched before his career advanced any distance at all, and the Gospel message carried abroad by so many others might have died on the road a hundred times over.

As it was, Paul found a good solid nucleus of Christianity in the imperial City, with Peter possibly there to receive him, and before long delegates from nearly all the churches Paul had organised in the east congregated round him to demonstrate their solidarity and store up his advice before he came to trial, with what upshot one could never foresee. Luke, Timothy, Mark stayed closed at hand. The *Acts* of Luke end with Paul 'preaching the kingdom of God, and teaching those things which concern the Lord Jesus Christ, with all confidence, no man forbidding him'.

Nobody knows whether Paul's trial came off at the end of the two years during which Luke shows him thus happily engaged. If it did, the upshot was favourable, for Paul's correspondence of 62–64 shows that he was then travelling again to Greece and Asia. But in 64 he reappeared in Rome as a prisoner, this time in gaol. Gaol was not itself a place of punishment, only a transit station for delinquents awaiting trial or execution, and so nothing at all was done to make it habitable; the prisons of antiquity did not lag behind the worst of any age, in point of harshness and squalor. The Roman prisons just then were packed with Christians. The two and a half centuries when martyrdom formed an integral part of Christian life-expectancy had begun.

Though the Empire as a whole was at peace, in the heart of it there was acute discontent with the person of Emperor Nero, whose murderous eccentricities threatened to surpass those of Caligula which they recalled. The glamour which surrounded him – a handsome and gilded young man – to start with, was dimmed first by military disaster in Britain and then by an eruption of Vesuvius, events which it was possible to attribute to the displeasure of the gods whom Nero

variously blasphemed. He would not be the first of his lineage to be
assassinated, a fact of which he was well aware and rightly nervous.
After the catastrophe of 19–25 July 64, when eleven out of the City's
fifteen districts were laid in ashes, public opinion, as always desiring
a definite agency to blame, quickly launched a spate of rumours that
Nero had set Rome on fire for amusement.

Nero did the best he could to scotch the rumours by extreme
generosity in the way of public relief and assistance – a generosity so
unprecedented that it merely served to convince the people of his
guilty conscience. The whys, wherefores, and hows remain matters
of surmise, but the fact is indubitable that the emperor decided to
divert suspicion from himself by fastening it on to the Christian sect,
vaguely arraigned for 'villainous practices and hatred towards the
whole human race'. It strikes a chord.

The emperor had the power and the necessary morbid, theatrical
inventiveness to harp upon that chord, the ever-rousing scapegoat
motif, with the utmost effect. The proof of crime is in the punishment
of it, and punishing the alleged fire-raisers was combined with fantastic
spectacles of atrocities such as took even the blood-loving Roman
theatre audiences' breath away. It all began with a gala hunt in the
imperial park, where Christians sewn into animal skins were torn to
pieces by mastiffs, followed by nocturnal illumination of the gardens
with human torches coated in pitch and resin, to continue with an
unendingly fertile repertoire of fanciful butchery at the circus. The
populace was duly diverted. Some were sickened by the surfeit of
human agony continually on display – Tacitus in passing questioned
the wisdom of it, as it seemed to him calculated to arouse pity – but
not enough to call a halt.

No popular uprising but only the usual palace revolution made an
end of Nero, four years after the fire. His demise did not bring the
Christian-baiting to an end. The name of Christian had become as
good as synonymous with moral leper and arena-victim. Together
with the built-in human need for scapegoats marches the need to feel
that the scapegoat deserves what it is getting. The more settled a
feature the persecutions became, the more hatred, contempt, and
calumny settled on the quarry.

Cannibalism ('This is my body, this is my blood'), incest, ritual sodomy and promiscuous orgies were among the charges preferred against the Christians. And since famine, epidemics and other calamities would always recur, there would always be renewed stimulus to reach for the scapegoat. It was easy to recoil with appropriate loathing from the filthy, debilitated creatures, ugly and stinking with ill-usage, that came up from the dungeons to their doom.

Many Christians indeed succumbed to panic or to torture, abjured their faith, confessed to preposterous crimes, denounced others, joined the hunters. But many more stayed firm and, still more astonishingly, continued the campaign of Christian recruitment, under daily risk of frightful suffering, with an ever-increasing roll of martyred saints.

One secret of their strength was that their predicament was voluntary. As Tertullian could still write, 'A man becomes a Christian: he is not born one.' All a man, or a woman, or a child needed to do to walk away free and hale, was to recant: just two or three words to that effect, the merest pinch of incense burnt before a heathen altar, would suffice. In not a few cases judge and executioner implored the victim thus to spare all concerned another ghastly incident – fruitlessly.

It became a part of the Christian combat training to discuss the deaths of friends and to prepare oneself to carry off the same pains and humiliations when the time came, '. . . that you may give proof of your faith, a much more precious thing than the gold which is assayed by fire,' as wrote Peter. Now was the long night of the catacombs.

Peter and Paul perished some time before the suicide of Nero, between 66–68. The Empire was not made safe for Christianity until 313, by the conversion to the faith of Emperor Constantine the Great; and in the intervening period the subterranean Christian cemeteries grew to vast proportions. In Rome alone, it is believed, large areas of them remain to be discovered. There are other catacombs in Tuscany, Sicily, Egypt, Africa and Asia Minor; those of Rome were the earliest founded and most extensive. The first one took its name from the locality of the entrance, and 'catacomb' eventually became a generic label.

Underground burial places were not a Christian invention; in Italy, particularly, great warrens of that type dated back to prehistoric times. But they came to unexampled development at the service of the Primitive Church. Veritable labyrinths of mile upon mile of

twisting, intersecting galleries, they were tunnelled through successive
strata of volcanic subsoil, sometimes with as many as seven storeys
above one another, accessible by narrow stairs, and ventilated by oc-
casional air shafts. The ceilings of the corridors were vaulted, sepulchral
niches excavated in the vertical walls, and parallel with them, like
many-tiered bunks, mostly to the number of five or six ranges, but
here and there rising to twelve ranges. Some compartments housed
one body each, some several, carefully sealed, to contain the gases of
decomposition, with slabs of marble or cemented tiles which were
often engraved or painted with epitaphs to the departed, by name or
as 'known to God alone'. Some tombs were more elaborate, protected
with marble grilles and placed in frescoed cubicles; some of the galleries
too were plastered over and decorated in bright colours, with flowers
and birds, biblical scenes, and symbols of the faith such as the fish
(*ichthus* in Greek, the five letters of that word giving *I*esus *Ch*restos
*Th*eou *Ui*os *S*oter = Jesus Christ, of God the Son, Saviour), the
Sacred Monogram formed by the initial letters of *Chrestos*, the dove
and olive branch of the Ark, the palm frond of rejoicing, the anchor of
hope, the lamb of sacrifice. Here and there larger chambers were excavated to accommodate specially distinguished saints, with sarcophagi
or table tombs that served as communion tables at the obsequies or
at those times when all places of pious assembly above ground were alike
unsafe; often little glass bottles with remnants of eucharistic wine
were cemented into the enclosure at the end of the funeral love feast.
But there were also graves simply dug into the floor, and false galleries
with blocked exits or secret openings into the countryside; these were
added when at the peak of the persecutions the leaders of the community
were kept in hiding down among the dead.

The gravediggers of the Christians who thus constructed an esti-
mated five hundred miles of necropolitan passages at Rome were men
of equal skill, courage and integrity, and were important members of
the congregation. In the midst of sustained cataclysm, a hierarchy was
taking shape.

6

The Ladder
of Sainthood

All believers were saints, but some were beginning to be accounted holier than others.

From the outset of their mission without the departed Master, there had been some implicit grading of authority, as the Twelve looked to their designated senior and everybody else looked to the Twelve. Somewhere democratic procedure had to stop, which it did in the dictates of the Holy Spirit, still manifesting itself through dreams and visions at moments of decision. Authority was delegated by formal blessing: by laying on of hands, as had been done with the first seven deacons of Jerusalem, in conformity with ancient biblical etiquette. This precedent was observed whenever new lieutenants were promoted in charge of churches organised by the apostles, and by these deputies in their turn. Nevertheless, in sanctity they and all the rank and file were equals, if only because it was their unity and union with the Christ that sanctified them.

Yet naturally the martyrs – they that underwent the baptism of fire, over and above baptism of water, testifying to the holy communion with their own bodies and blood over and above the mystic ingestion once a week of the body and blood of the Saviour – achieved a special degree of consecration. God knew they deserved to be honoured among the brethren left behind. Man cannot live in brotherhood alone, nor solely by the model of a superhuman entity; he must have heroes, too, in his own image.

The apostles expected to be martyred, unless Jesus returned first. The two Jameses had led the way, both of them at Jerusalem, before the Roman persecutions were launched in which Peter and Paul were gathered to their Master. Paul died by the sword, beheaded as was his privilege as a Roman citizen. Peter, about to escape from Rome during the Neronic massacres, met the Lord on the road and enquired where he was going. 'To Rome, to be crucified again,' the Lord replied;

Sixth-century ivory Coptic panels representing the four Evangelists, with the Healing of the Paralytic and Christ and the Woman of Samaria shown above. Coptics is the name given to the early native Christians of Egypt and their descendant sectaries.

Primeval innocence and eternal hope: ivory diptych *c.* 400, showing, on the left, Adam as lord of creation before the fall, and, on the right, scenes from St Paul's ministry on the island of Malta.

St Paul: a mid-fourth-century fresco from the catacomb of Praetextatus.

St Andrew, after Francesco Parmigiano (1503–47). The patron saint of Scotland, he was martyred at Patras by crucifixion on an X-shaped cross.

Synthesis: statue of St Peter, now in the Vatican grottoes. A thirteenth-century head was grafted on a classical marble body, with the further, fourteenth-century addition of the hands holding the symbolic crossed keys.

opposite Mid-sixth-century mosaic of St Peter and St Damian in the church of Cosmas and Damian, Rome.

St Simon the Apostle, martyred, according to tradition, in Persia, with a basket of fishes, his emblem in art. From a painting of a stained-glass window in the Guildhall, Norwich.

centre St Thomas the apostle. It is claimed in the *Acts of Thomas*, a third-century Christian manuscript, that it was Thomas who took the Gospel to India, and that he was martyred there. From the Guildhall, Norwich.

top right St Bartholomew the apostle, possibly the same man as Nathanael, whose emblem is the butcher's knife with which he was flayed; and St James the apostle, often represented, as here, as a pilgrim, with the cockleshell bag and staff carried by the pilgrims to his most famous shrine at Santiago de Compostiela. From Ranworth Church, Norfolk.

bottom right St Jude the apostle, reputed author of the last epistle in the New Testament, here carrying a ship, frequently used as a symbol of the Church of Christ which, like Noah's Ark, safely rides the deluge; St Matthew, apostle, evangelist and author of the first gospel. From Ranworth Church, Norfolk.

St Michael the Archangel, traditionally the guardian of the sick and receiver of the souls of the dead, is here depicted weighing souls. From a church window at Martham, Norfolk.

St Mark the Evangelist

St Matthew overcoming the forces of evil

and Peter turned back to meet his fate. Condemned to crucifixion, he held himself unworthy of dying in the same posture as Jesus, and was granted his request that it be done upside down.

Peter, who had thrice denied Jesus at the time of the Master's arrest, doubtless was in a class by himself; in general, saints were enjoined not to court martyrdom or to make heroic gestures for the gesture's sake. Other apostles were permitted to escape and carry on their missions a little longer. Always, in the absence of definite information as to how they had finally come by their deaths, martyrdom was presumed. Even John, who died full of years among reverent friends at Ephesus, in after days was said to have gone back to Rome for martyrdom but to have emerged unharmed from a cauldron of boiling oil. Andrew the brother of Peter, lost sight of in Greece, was said to have died on an X-shaped cross in Patras. Matthias also was said to have been crucified – somewhere in Roman dominions. Bartholomew disappeared in Armenia, and was said to have been flayed alive. Simon the Zealot may have gone to Egypt and Persia, where he was said to have been martyred in company with Jude. Matthew also was said to have been martyred, in Persia – or possibly in Ethiopia. Luke died in Greece at the age of 84; Barnabas had died, probably on Cyprus, years before Paul or Peter appeared in Rome, and like Luke was eventually allotted putative martyrdom. Mark may or may not have been martyred in Alexandria, where he was the first bishop of the district church: when the flock was everywhere suffering so much, it became in a manner unbelievable that the shepherds might have been spared the cruel glory; in a manner it was an unwitting courtesy gesture to make them, as it were, honorary martyrs, whether or no. As with the cross of Jesus, the instrument of execution in most cases became the different martyrs' emblems.

There were, then, bishops (overseers) now as well as deacons (servants) and presbyters (elders) of the Church. A new priesthood was developing, before the dream of the saints came true in any country to have a church, a house of worship, expressly built and exclusively devoted to that purpose. Not until well on in the second century was there ever enough money or a long enough lull in the anti-Christian campaign to erect such edifices. Meanwhile the growing congregations made shift as best they could, where possible in the villas of their richer members, the standard layout of which was, as it happened, very suitable for Christian assembly. For example, the entrance hall where guests were commonly received provided an outer court for catechumens, the inner court was for full, baptised members; the antechamber to the private apartments served as a kind of prototypal vestry, and the dining room was the obvious place for the central ceremony of the cult, the sacred meal.

Somebody had to administer the meal, somebody had to speak the opening and closing formulae, somebody had to give instruction to catechumens, baptise those ready for it, lead the prayers, choose what passages were to be read. The ceremony later to be called the mass, in its original form began with the invocation of God's mercy, next amplified in collective prayers of the faithful. Then came the reading – from the Old Testament, the *Torah*, current apostolic instructions, or some account of a recent martyrdom, with psalm-singing in between. This part of the service was for everybody, including interested visitors. It ended with the official leader of the congregation facing it with arms outstretched and the words which have not changed, 'The Lord be with you. Let us pray.' The congregation prayed standing, not with their hands placed together but with their arms outstretched in the position of the cross. After another collect, catechumens, penitents, and visitors were dismissed. Now the sacrificial donations were made: the bread and the wine to be consecrated, and contributions to the relief fund for the poor and the bereaved of the community. The minister then prayed the Almighty to accept the people's worldly gifts and grant in exchange the gifts of heaven, and, inviting the faithful to rejoice in experiencing the mystery now to be re-enacted, stretched out his hands over the bread and wine, pronounced the words of Jesus at the Last Supper which transformed the ordinary foodstuffs into the sacred elements, and finally asked all to come forward and share the meal. Afterwards there was collective thanksgiving, at the end of which the faithful knelt to receive the blessing, with the conclusion, 'Go, it is finished' – the phrase that in its Latin rendering of, 'Ite, missa est', is in some quarters thought to be the origin of the word 'mass'.

The word pontiff, derived from the 'pontifex' of pagan Roman priesthood, was as yet foreign to the Greek-speaking Primitive Church, even as the notion of a Christian priestly caste was yet unthought of – Paul had distinctly declared that Christ was the only high priest of his saints, every one of whom was qualified to communicate and minister. Paul had on the whole continued to favour the Jewish tradition, which preferred teachers to have a manual trade for subsistence. Others however opposed to this Jesus' dictum, 'The labourer is worthy of his hire' (given to allay the scruples of the disciples when, as wandering teachers unable to ply a trade, they found themselves having to be supported by the communities they visited). A similar situation arose in the settled Christian churches, since by reason of growth both in membership and persecution it often became impossible for the leading officials to make their own livings. They, like the sick, the crippled, the widows and the orphans, necessarily came to be maintained by the community, and in that sense began to form a professional class as yet without the name of such.

It was inevitable that accounts of the martyrdom of leaders distinguished in the community, and usually singled out for especially ghastly treatment which they met with corresponding nobility of conduct, figured prominently in the sacred lists from which selection was made for the readings during the first part of community worship. Those many, poor, nameless martyrs, destroyed beyond identification in obscure torture chambers without even the staying challenge of public witness – truly they were as venerable as the ones whom men could put a name to. All the same, human memory was better served, fidelity better strengthened by the example of martyrs whose names and stories were known and kept green by recital. What was more natural than that the survivors who had loved them should perennially revisit their graves and cherish souvenirs of their obsequies ? What more natural, in those periods when nocturnal Christian worship was reduced entirely to the catacombs, than to hold meetings at the graveside of some such hero ? And what more natural than to send special greetings to the deity through the person who had already ascended to bliss and whose remains presided over the occasion ?

Paul quite early on listed three categories of leader: apostles, prophets, and teachers, graded in that order; in his own person he had combined all three. He had not specifically mentioned officials, but these now often doubled the roles of prophet and teacher. Missionaries of course were by definition on the move and not to be tied down to one particular cell.

The gift of prophecy was not primarily equated with foretelling future events on earth but with things eternal; the voice of God poured from his mouthpieces without thought or volition on their part. Inspired and inspiring, prophets diffused a state of mind rather than information.

The teachers soon went beyond imparting information under the new discipline. They followed in the steps of the Jewish Doctors of the Law and the Greek philosophers, rivalling and supplanting these in the appropriate circles, and so to some extent the heirs of both. The basic difference, that they applied established modes of thought to a novel ideology, could not but affect the intellectual method itself. To begin with, the word *gnosis*, relating to knowledge, wisdom, just like its Latin successor *scientia*, merely signified the pursuit of deeper understanding, without any reference to heresy on the one hand or exploration of Nature on the other, with which in the form of Gnosticism and Science they would respectively become associated in the far future. With the lives of the first generation of apostles the scrip-

tures, held to be of direct divine inspiration, came to an end and
human exegesis took over. The 'Fathers of the Church' were the
scholars and interpreters of Christian gnosis.

Again, in the beginning the term Father was the standard appellation
of the bishops, although later the collective honorific would become
exclusive to the most influential theologians of Christianity of the first
four centuries, and the singular (via *pappas*, *papa*, Pope) would descend
likewise exclusively upon the bishop of Rome, within the orbit of
Western Christendom. There was to be no split of East and West for
over a thousand years; and diversity indeed was sanctioned if not
always welcomed as a fruitful stimulant. Paul had said, 'There must
be sects', – as a kind of scale-marker, in his meaning, by which to
measure the perspective of Truth.

Miracle-workers in the flesh were getting rarer during a period
when demonstrations of the Messianic power were most notably by
personal sacrifice. Jesus had not used his power to save himself, Peter's
and Paul's miraculous escapes from prison had not been enacted by
themselves but by angels that rescued them so that they might be
able to complete their work. Imperviousness, like the apostle John's
to boiling oil, was exceptional (but he, too, had yet had to write the
Apocalypse and the Fourth Gospel). Even in the accounts of James
the Less and of Sebastian – the former surviving a fall from a great
height, the latter healed after having been shot full of arrows – both
saints later succumbed to clubbing to death. The same pattern occurs
again and again in the deaths of martyrs: miraculous invulnerability,
showing that the saint could save himself if he would, followed by
submission to mortality at the next attempt to execute him.

The sacrifice was an essential part of spiritual victory. Posthumous
miracles, however, showing up the spuriousness of physical death,
became a telling mark of sainthood. People found healing at the graves
of saints or relief from demons that had possessed them – just as healing
and exorcism had been the main acts in this direction of Jesus and the
disciples. A symbolic, parabolic, as it were solemnly playful interpretation was possible with regard to wonders worked upon human
victuals, as at the marriage of Cana and the miracle of the loaves and
fishes, but not when it came to raising the dead, making cripples walk and
skin diseases disappear, and freeing poor souls from parasitic evil spirits.

At the graves of some saints, or by contact with relics of them, more cures and exorcisms were vouchsafed than through the agency of others. Sometimes the manner of their martyrdom, and thus the emblems of their passion, made possible some sympathetic specialisation – so that Apollonia, who had had her teeth torn out, was invoked against tooth-ache; Lucy, who had plucked out her own eyes in order to discourage an importunate lover, was invoked against ophthalmic complaints; Agatha whose breasts had been clipped off with shears was appealed to by sufferers afflicted in that part of the body; and so forth.

Conjuring thaumaturgy, such as transforming an ordinary object into something else, or plucking objects out of thin air, levitation, absence of putrefaction after death or a scent of roses supplanting the odour of death, did not enter the picture till centuries later. This was the sort of thing associated with pagan magic (stringently forbidden in the Old Testament). To be sure, healing and exorcism played a part in pagan magic too, as did, for that matter, love feasts centring on a divine resurrection. But the difference here was that the rites in question were symbolic of natural phenomena, such as the cycle of the year, the waning and waxing of the moon, or were observed purely in a spirit of propitiation; with suspension of the laws of nature serving merely to attest the powers of the priestly magician-demonstrator.

In Christianity, the whole point of miracles was that they were not 'magic' in that sense, but didactic manifestations of the omnipotence of God, concrete tokens that the heavenly kingdom was attained by saints who had joined him, while the sacred meal of holy communion signified just that: the fraternal union of believers in communion with God. The stress on the total interrelation and reciprocity of humanity and godhead was constant and all-pervading.

Saints were human. They were not all of them capable of living up to the saintly standards, all of the time. Quite apart from those who defected, or worse, under pressure of the terror, even the staunchest were subject like all men to fault and sin and error – ranging from anger and inability to love one's enemies or opportunist compromises with a hostile environment to the civil crimes of theft, perjury, adultery, murder. When they committed any of these, they automatically fell from saintliness. There was at one time a move to exclude them from the brotherhood for ever, but in view of Jesus' forbearance towards repentant sinners, this was dropped. However, repentance was the operative factor of re-admission. The sinner had to be purified before he became eligible again.

Purification was by penitence, *vis-à-vis* the community which the sinner had flawed as well as the deity he had offended; the change of heart to which he had testified in the baptismal ceremony of rebirth would have to be evidenced afresh. Clearly restitution had to be preceded by confession, and some person other than the sinner himself must adjudicate. Thus public confession came into being, attended by suspension from the community of saints until a given sentence of penances had been performed and the bishop formally consecrated the return of the outcast.

The slaking of conscience which was thus experienced, the feeling of having cleared all one's debts, was so obviously beneficial that by degrees the principle of penitence gained further ground. Where shortcomings were a matter of the heart only introspection could bring them to light – inexorably revealing a bottomless pit of inborn iniquity, unsuspected till one buckled down to stripping the successive layers of consciousness. Try as he would, no man was so good that he could altogether avoid sinning in his heart. Logically, it was impossible to keep up with one's sins which sprang from an inexhaustible source of guilt – the guilt incurred by Adam and Eve. Saints began to atone not only for sins they were already conscious of but also for those which continuous delving was bound continuously to uncover, so long as they dwelt in their mortal bodies.

Some therefore embraced a lifetime of penitence, chasing peace while yet they lived, and always one step behind. Penances consisted mainly of privations and humiliating exercises, together with extra devotions. Asceticism was not a new thing among either Jews or pagans, to whom such purgative austerities were indeed well known as means of casting off material concerns and inducing states of heightened spiritual sensibility. But again in the Christian context asceticism acquired a new dimension. The subject's evidently profound sense of unworthiness, and his utter, advance surrender to the world Beyond, placed him on a no less heroic level than that of the blood witness – more especially so when the persecutions abated.

Sainthood, hitherto a group characteristic, turned into a title of

The dedication of the first Christian Church

respect for individuals who earned particular reverence. The anniver-
saries of their release from mortal toils and ascension to glory – whether
by martyrdom or natural causes – were celebrated not as days of
mourning but feasts of triumph and joy. Their intercession was sought
by those still living – intercession as yet merely by way of a prayerful
good word put in with the deity. Their names were piously perpetuated,
now adopted in baptism by admirers hoping to be like them, now in
dedicating a church to their memory.

The first saint known to have been honoured at a regular annual
feast was Polycarp, bishop of Smyrna, martyred at the stake about 155
at the age of at least ninety years: 'I have served him for eighty-six
years and he has done me no harm,' Polycarp replied when urged to
curse Christ; whereupon his pyre was kindled.

'He looked, not like burning flesh, but like bread in the oven or gold
and silver being refined in a furnace,' the church of Smyrna wrote to
a sister-congregation in Phrygia, thus also furnishing the first, written
eye-witness account of a Christian martyrdom since that of Stephen.
All other accounts of martyrs in the intervening one hundred and

A saint holding the cross: detail from a third-century Coptic relief.

St George, legendary fourth-century martyr, and patron saint of England. From Ketteringham Church, Norfolk.

top left St Agnes, *d. c.* 300, whose emblem is a lamb. One of the most celebrated Roman martyrs, she was killed by being stabbed in the throat. From Ranworth Church, Norfolk.

left St Barbara, patroness of gunners and miners, whose emblems are a tower representing her place of incarceration as well as symbolising the Trinity, and a plume or phoenix's feather commemorating her birthplace of Heliopolis. From Ketteringham Church, Norfolk.

St Apollonia, patroness of dentists,
depicted with her emblem, a forceps
gripping a tooth, and St Zita, patroness
of domestic servants, with her emblem,
a bunch of keys. From a screen
painting in Barton Church, Norfolk.

St Margaret of Antioch, from an early fifteenth-century Book of Hours.
Although there is no documentary evidence of her existence, legend has it
that she was the daughter of a pagan priest and was swallowed by Satan in
the form of a dragon. She was martyred by beheading.

Cette beste naint les sainz & hyperne laorent

St Lawrence and the seven-headed beast of the Apocalypse, from an early fourteenth-century French manuscript. Note the flames of his gridiron, the instrument of his martyrdom, in the bottom right-hand corner.

St Gregory, St Basil, and St John Chrysostom, three of the great teachers
of the Eastern Church. A mosaic from Capella Palatina, Palermo.

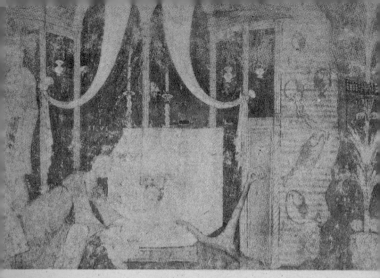

St (Pope) Sylvester led into Rome in triumph by Constantine, after the latter's conversion to Christianity: fresco dated 1246 in the Oratory of St Sylvester, SS Quattro Coronati, Rome.

top St Clement, reputedly among St Peter's first successors in the see of Rome, here shown miraculously sustaining a child's life in his underwater shrine. Eleventh-twelfth-century fresco in St Clemente lower church, Rome.

twenty years survived only in the form of 'legends', that is, hieratic reading matter for public recitation on the feast day of the saint so celebrated. Such accounts were not necessarily 'legendary' in the latter-day sense of that word, but being stylised and polished for ecclesiastical use, they could never rank as affidavits.

At the same time as saints and church functionaries acquired graduated status, so did the church communities themselves. The bishoprics from being initially congregational, so that each church however small was an episcopate, evolved into diocesan institutions, with one bishop overseeing a whole group of churches in a particular district. These enlarged, centralised episcopates in turn obeyed the hierarchic trend; with the result that the largest and most important became known as patriarchates. Of these the first and foremost were Rome, Jerusalem, Antioch, Alexandria and Byzantium; and the greatest of them, again, with the widest jurisdiction, was Rome – hallowed as the ancient see of Peter the appointed deputy of Jesus, and by the blood of Peter, Paul, and the vast majority of the martyrs.

7

The Missionaries

The Jewish state had become defunct in AD 70, when Jerusalem fell and the Temple was razed. Only the Temple tax, which Jews throughout the world had contributed towards the upkeep of the central sanctuary, was not rescinded: the Roman government appropriated it. Possibly this was an ancillary reason for Rome's hostility to the early Christian dissidents who no longer considered themselves Jews and thus robbed the imperial exchequer by default. But for its being the site of the Passion and the cradle of the faith, Jerusalem would scarcely have rated a patriarchate. Jerusalem was the rallying point of the Jewish-Palestinian churches, inward-looking rather than straining outward, and still looking somewhat askance at the churches of the Gentiles, who returned the compliment. Future anti-semitism had been seeded, and the vital Christian impetus had passed over to the Gentiles. One might go so far as to say that in the third and fourth centuries Palestine was re-colonised here and there by Gentile religious settlers of Christian persuasion.

This was the case particularly with hermits and anchorite groups which, gradually filtering through from Egypt where the vogue probably had its inception, found in the awesome immensity of the desert places and matching skies the same compulsion that had sent the ancient Israelites on their search for God.

Since it was the general directive for Christians during the persecutions to save themselves if they could without apostasy, the first Christian hermits were isolated fugitives who went to earth in the handy caves and wilderness round about the Red Sea. Necessity became a virtue: sexual continence, abstention from meat, intoxicating drink and worldly comforts and interests became the objects of deliberate vows. The ancient idea of ascetic retreat for propitiatory, contemplative, or hallucinatory ends began to be systematised, just as had the ancient sacerdotal features of communal feasting and gastronomic mime. Without the spur of necessity, men and women took to voluntary retirement from mundane distractions and lived as permanent prisoners to God. Often they chose tombs or disused wells for their prisons and showed remarkable longevity. However, many perished untimely in complete solitude where they were the helpless prey equally of ruinous depressions and bodily perils. Thus it came about that some hermits banded together, dwelling each in his own small, confined shelter, but assembling for daily devotions and periodical theological discussions, and living communally off the land, such as it was. They allowed themselves out on parole for works of charity.

The two Egyptian saints Antony and Pachomius, whose lives and works overlapped, though not in association, figure as the prototypes of Christian monasticism, but they were not the first. They were however the most prominent and so most influential organisers of collective hermitages in the sands of their country. The Antonine type remained basically individualistic, with a widely spaced scattering of recluses acknowledging one spiritual director. The Pachomian type was thoroughly collective and institutionalised, enclosed in restricted villages, with all activities strictly regulated.

Thus from havens of pure contemplation these hermitages grew into what were termed 'schools for the service of God'. More than that, they grew into centres of advice and instruction to the laity. Christianity from having been a predominantly urban movement began to spread at last in earnest among the *pagani*, the people of the countryside. Innumerable variant offshoots sprang from the twin-stem of Antony and Pachomius, and proliferated with incredible speed.

The Devil himself complained bitterly to St Antony that the desert, for ages past the acknowledged stamping ground of demons, was swarming with holy hermits nowadays – and the Devil had seen nothing yet: that was only the start. The surprising popularity of a way of life which some contemporary critics classed as 'worse than the existence of a pig', and which not a few bishops viewed with considerable reserve, might be partially explained by the fact that all the time the Second Advent was expected, if not tomorrow or the next day, at least in the foreseeable future. Devout believers felt they could hardly wait; and taking to the desert perhaps seemed the equivalent of standing ready with one's spiritual bags packed for instant departure when the moment came. Gradually monastic colonies and wandering hermits fairly overran all the wide open spaces of the Middle East, as well as staking claims near most of the important places named in Scripture; and finally they also invaded the West, via Rome.

But by then Christianity had won toleration, indeed positive ascendancy, in the Empire. It had entered official history following the conversion of Emperor Constantine, and the seal of recognition had retrospective effect. Large as loomed the era of growth under oppression in the annals of the faithful, their sufferings and achievements had so far attracted only passing notice in the world at large. Although martyrs in their thousands had died public deaths, the development of their abused and hunted sect had remained a kind of private chronicle. Now, blazoned forth into the open, that hitherto obscure sectarian progress chart would be actually superimposed on the political records, so that all the emphasis was shifted and the past took on a new look in the light of hindsight, which picked out a different pattern. Hagiography, suddenly, *was* history, and the monasteries became the principal clearing houses of that commodity. For, notably by the influence of Basil the Great (330–79), bishop of Caesaraea, monasticism had become linked with literature and education besides divine and social services.

Basil and his friends established what was in effect a new town, complete with its own church, at Neocaesaraea, which included such amenities as alms houses, a hospice for travellers, a hospital having resident physicians and nurses and farmers and artisans attached, and an academy, all under monastic auspices. While this scheme remained unique in scope and scale for many a long day, it nevertheless acted as a widely valid model. Diluted but unmistakable, the conceptions of Basil formed a part of the equipment of the new missionaries to the West.

The earliest of these were lost in the mists of time – the mists, in truth, of those vast tracts of virgin forest and primeval marshes covering transalpine Europe. The fervent enthusiasm and astounding physical hardihood of the desert-bred evangelists carried them untold distances. Some authorities believe that Paul's remark in the second epistle to Timothy, 'Crescens has gone to Galatia', should read, 'to Gaul'. While definite information is lacking as to how the gospel rumours first got around in the remote regions of Gaul, Germany, Britain, Scandinavia, there can be no doubt that such rumours were already current long before those mission stations were established that we know by name or through the names of their most distinguished products – Patrick, Aidan, Columba, Boniface, Martin of Tours. All these men had got an already solid Christian background, and had been educated and trained at monasteries in their own or immediately neighbouring countries.

Among the Barbarians the efforts of their first evangelists were, once again, the merest episodes – now giving pause for wonder as some chieftain accepted baptism, now swelling some local stock of sanguinary anecdotes, according to whether the evangelist succeeded or failed. Many vanished without trace or echo. But very evidently they always came again.

They came, on foot, by boat, in pairs according to apostolic tradition or in little troops, with the baggage of merchant caravans, as camp followers or even members of the army, as slaves brought to market by the pirate raiders of the northern seas who knew nothing of the Mediterranean *Pax Romana*. The zone of martyrdom shifted to the hinterlands of civilisation. Still, here the incidence was only sporadic. Martyrdom was no longer the Christian's ineluctable portion, but simply an occupational hazard of the missionary activist.

What had the heralds of the oriental Christ to offer in these outer reaches? in societies that though beyond the nomad stage were still organised primarily for tribal warfare and hunting? to people whose thinking was all earth-bound, blood-bound, action-bound; whose morality rested entirely in material prowess; with whom slaves were incidental chattels, not an industrial foundation; where wealth was gold and weapons and plenty to eat and drink rather than improved comforts in general; where women though unfranchised enjoyed an archaic respect; and where men were quite happy with their crude but adequate religions?

Superstition is the name we give to beliefs and practices discredited in our own outlook, to our certain knowledge as we feel. In cognitions and indigenous skills the Barbarians were not very far above the pre-historic level; and they were extremely superstitious. Nurtured in absolute physical fearlessness, their universe, consisting altogether

of rationally unexplained phenomena, surrounded them with supernatural terror. It might be nothing to them that somewhere in the
unimaginable East a man had died on the cross and come back to life –
as for gods surmounting ritual execution, they had some of those themselves – and they might see no point in an after-life that was not all
happy hunting grounds and inexhaustible banqueting; but anything
unusual, from the simplest conjuring trick to portentous coincidence,
easily prostrated them with awe.

The first reaction to awe is not usually love but hatred. These people
were not cowards, they lashed out at what they feared, killing was their
universal remedy. But, although as often as not honoured in the
breach as in the observance, loyalty was the supreme good in their
ethic. To violate a promise or the bonds of fidelity was the greatest
wrong they recognised, which they believed to be justly visited with
utter rejection, here and Beyond. Once a Barbarian had sworn allegiance
to the new God, he quite often kept faith with that God's representa-
tives – particularly as his previous adherence to his native deities was
seldom a matter of outright personal dedication. Much depended on
what had induced him to strike the metaphysical bargain – whether
the cause was of sufficient magnitude.

If his life had been saved, or the life of his family and tribe, if a
battle had been won against heavy odds, a flood stayed, a storm halted,
contrary winds reversed or a deadly calm ended by a crucial breeze –
then it would undoubtedly be very dangerous to go back on the bargain.
But if, for any such reason, one's chief had made the compact binding
on his people as well as his own self without their individual consent,
then any unwilling converts might some time or other consider themselves entitled to revert from it. For sickness, fatality, famine and other
disasters did not perish from the earth forever under the sign of the
cross; the old gods were not rendered so impotent by the new that they
forbore from revenge. As many people thought the missionaries brought
bad luck as had grounds for gratitude towards them.

Lasting Christianisation was a much slower process in the West,
even where language barriers were still bridged under the Roman
aegis, be it only by camp-Latin. But given time to make themselves
useful, the evangelists not infrequently struck root. Where they could,
they fed the hungry, nursed the stricken, cleared fresh land for hus-

Allegory of the clergy and the laity on the troubled waters of life

bandry, and introduced such utilitarian arts and crafts as commended themselves to these culturally undemanding heathen. Education for its own sake cut very little ice – as witness the cautionary legend of St Cassian, stabbed to death by his pupils with their iron pens.

Miracles continued to be the missionary's best stock in trade, as convincing to himself in the ardour of his faith, in the ambiguous climate of these dark, dank territories, in charismatic rapture, as they were to his audiences. St Columba banished a water monster from the river Ness (little thinking that the creature would merely bide its time in the adjoining loch); St Boniface made the herring return to the nets of the starving fisherfolk of Friesland; St Cuthbert was an able resurrectionist especially of young children; St Martin saved many a harvest.

The miracles of the missionaries were what the hagiographers concentrated on and what their public most liked to read or hear about. Edification was considered of greater moral value and more interesting than circumstantial accuracy. The people preferred their 'holy athletes' to defeat giants and dragons, to compel the affections of wild beasts and serpents, to speak the language of the birds, walk on the water or through fire, make mountains open and shut or turn a gnawed bone

into a whole roast sucking pig – to having them display merely spiritual
and psychological powers.

Even so, missionaries continued to be murdered and the converted
heathen went on backsliding.

The most decisive step towards stabilising the situation was taken
by that brilliant organising genius, St Gregory, surnamed the Great
(c. 540–604), first pope of his name and the first monk ever to be elected
in the succession to St Peter, who extended the area of Christendom
and the authority of the Roman see as never before. Pope Gregory
suggested to the European missionaries that, instead of burning down
the heathen sanctuaries and anathematising heathen festivals, they
should convert those abominations to Christian use – as far as possible
making temples into churches, building chapels in sacred groves or
under sacred trees, and celebrating the Lord's birthday at the feast of
the winter solstice. Why not, since Easter had in any case occurred at
a spring festival in Palestine and Whitsun at a harvest festival? The
wisdom of the stratagem was soon proved. The death rate of missionaries went down. Heathen who had bloodily defended their
sanctuaries against destruction were more likely to give in to mere
renovations which the old gods themselves did not take the trouble to
demolish, and it was easier to clean up their festivals than to abolish
them. Synchronising of feasts and Christian trimmings to old places of
worship facilitated new habits.

But the heathen deities got their own back in some respects. In the
course of time some of the dispossessed nymphs, demigods and gods
also became converted for good measure. They became naturalised
saints, reappearing – first in folk tales, and then in Christian re-inter-
pretations of obsolescent iconography – in the guise of mythical
martyrs who were trustfully venerated in the places of forgotten,
fallen idols. The subject is a controversial one, but the list of saints
without any trace of historical existence is not meagre. Apart from
touching inventions like St Mercury and more than one mythical St
Hermes, several pairs of brothers bearing a strong resemblance to the
Dioscuri (including one pair named Sergius and Bacchus), and crypto-
Aphrodites like Pelagia of Tarsus and Marina, some of the most popular
saints after the Dark Ages – like St Roch, St Philomena, St Ursula,
and even the indestructible St Sebastian among others – were in the

'The Temptation of St Antony', by Martin Schongauer (*c.* 1445–*c.* 1488),
a painter most noted and influential in the field of engraving. St Antony
spent most of his life as a desert hermit and is regarded as one of the fathers
of monasticism, traditionally associated with the persistent, violent
spiritual and physical temptations which he had to overcome.

An eleventh–twelfth-century pyx showing the martyrdom of St Menas. One of the most popular Egyptian saints, he was martyred c. 303 under Diocletian.

St Helena, mother of Emperor Constantine the Great, discovering the true cross at Jerusalem: the first instance of religiously inspired archaeology. Fresco dated 1246 in the Oratory of St Sylvester, SS Quattro Coronati, Rome.

Christ between Peter and Paul, above the divine lamb standing on a knoll from which spring the four rivers of Paradise (Pison, Gihon, Tigris, Euphrates – also symbolic of the four gospels), between SS Peter, Marcellinus, Gorgonius and Tiburtius. Late fourteenth-century relief in the Crypt of the Saints, catacomb of St Peter and St Marcellinus in Rome.

Michelangelo's 'Crucifixion of St Peter' in the Capella Paolina of the Vatican Palace, Rome: fresco executed between 1542 and 1550 for Pope Paul III.

course of time seen to be unsubstantiated figments. By that time, however, it was often impractical to abolish the cults of such saints: they had become too real and responsive; for faith, even if it cannot get blood out of a stone, can yet breathe life into it.

Even when the old gods were not integrated, they were hard to kill. They were demoted but not wiped out of existence. As evil spirits they joined the hordes of hell, like the Phoenician Baal Sebub, or Beelzebub, before them, and the '*Demon* Diana' (i.e. not 'the figment' Diana) of the classical apostolic age.

And these were not the only changes taking place in the ranks and condition of sainthood. Not only were some saints holier than others, now, but some were less holy than others – very much less holy, downright unholy, some of them. These latter were the dissidents, promoters of minority opinions within the Christian creed, the heretics, schismatics, minions of Satan.

A saint was no longer anybody who believed wholeheartedly in Jesus the Messiah. A saint had to be somebody who believed in Jesus Christ in the right way, who was included after death in an orthodox canon, and who had himself supernatural powers.

8
Cultus and Cultivation of Sainthood

The elements of the faith were all laid down in the Holy Scriptures, a canon which was now closed. But even aside from errors and distortions which inevitably slipped in as the sacred texts were copied over and over, fresh commentaries were continually added. Just as history needs to be periodically rewritten, so the Scriptures had to be explained to successive generations. Beset by hostile forces, it was necessary for Christianity to hammer out a firm line of orthodoxy, if it was not to splinter into fragments doomed by their disunity. Between them the Fathers of the Church saw to this – notably the four 'Greek Doctors' of the East, Athanasius (296–373), Gregory of Nazianzus (329–89), Basil the Great (c. 330–70), and John Chrysostom (347–407), and their counterparts of the West, the 'Latin Doctors' Hilary of Poitiers (c. 315–67), Ambrose (c. 334–97), Jerome (c. 342–420), and Augustine (354–430). They all have the prefix of Saint, and span the period of the greatest inter-Christian ideological battle until the Reformation.

Raging for a hundred years, the battle was launched about 321 by an Alexandrian priest named Arius (c. 260–336) who saw the whole principle of monotheism threatened by the doctrine of the Trinity, and though ceded to Jesus' divine attributes and every right of veneration, denied the Saviour's essential divinity.

Arius' teaching was condemned at the first general council of the Christian churches, convoked at Nicaea in 325, but the crisis which it had occasioned was not so simply settled and rent the Church from top to bottom, no sooner than it had come up for air from the era of persecution. It was largely through the work of the eight great Doctor Saints that the Arian Heresy was finally defeated before contention and bloodshed mounted to a climax of religious shooting-war.

But that was far from being the end of heresy. Hand in hand with the age of catholicism the heyday of heresies had opened. Though the name of Eastern heresy was scarcely less than legion, fundamentally it always hinged on the nature of the godhead and the constitution of the Trinity, unendingly fruitful of philosophical analysis. Never before or since was theological theory so universally gripping a topic. The butcher, the baker, the candlestick-maker bloodied one another's noses over the finer points, political factions rose and fell by the semantic niceties, palace intrigue and assassinations flourished on the ground of religious obstrusities.

The trouble with heresy was that almost invariably it sprang from the very highest motives, and also from the highest intellects. Orthodoxy, categorically lifting faith above the sphere of ratiocination, eventually carried the day – but not without carrying away infusions of heretical thought. The most potent dose, strangely enough, came from the least congenerous of sources, namely from Persian Magism. Named Manichaeism after its founder Mani (crucified AD 275 in Persia), this system contrived to accommodate ideas from virtually every type of cultus known to man, within the Christian framework. But the dominant ingredient was the Magian thesis of comprehensive dualism, by which Good and Evil had distinct and equal co-existence, locked in combat until such time as one or the other should conquer forever.

In Judaeo-Christian thought, good and evil were parts of one divine scheme, at war in human nature but not specifically residing in objective phenomena. In Manichaean thought the whole universe was divided into the two camps, not just symbolically but literally. All things were actual and partisan. Light *was* good, darkness *was* evil, God made the spirit, the Devil made the flesh. While this impaired God's position of almighty Creator, it did at last place his unalloyed benevolence beyond question and, so to speak, explained everything else. The practical conclusion to be drawn was that only by total annihilation of the material world could the ultimate conquest of evil be effected; hence man must assist God by abrogating the material world entirely, to inhibit its perpetuation.

Christian asceticism got a vigorous fillip from the uncompromising Manichaean logic. Already there had grown up a massive school of thought in favour of celibacy as an imperative adjunct of holiness, on a par with fasting and self-mortification, irrespective of penitence or intensified spiritual receptivity. That school now gained cumulative weight and thrust.

The apostles, most of whom were married men, had done no more than admit on occasion that family ties could be a distraction or a brake, and affirm that charitable self-denial is a godly virtue. The countless martyrs had done no more than apply the biological law of survival by which the future of the race has absolute priority over the life of the individual: they had died that the movement as a whole might live. Now, under the creeping toxaemia of Manichaeism, self-denial and self-immolation ceased to serve altruistic ends and were well on the way to becoming ends in themselves.

From rejecting personal survival in the interests of generic survival, saints progressed to rejecting biological survival altogether. From resisting the distractions of the world they progressed to denying that anything in it could be beautiful or good. Matter was the soul's prison, the flesh was its enemy. A fighting creed had forged indelible conventions. When the one-time underground movement became legitimised, its momentum turned from defence to attack. As social hostility lost striking power, the Force of Evil took its place. By identifying Evil with something tangible – with the very essence of concreteness, Matter – it was rendered that much easier to grapple with. The Manichaean principle which relieved a benign Creator of responsibility for everything unpleasant encouraged the perennial rebellion of thinking man against his inseverable bondage to the animal processes of the flesh, to unprecedented peaks of exaltation.

No longer hauled into the circus arena by human tormentors, saints found their jousting venue in their own bodies. If matter be the essence of evil, the essence of matter is reproduction, the sexual instinct the essence of carnality, to which health and strength, eating and excreting are but subservient. Anticipating a twentieth century which they never thought the world would live to see, the new wave of ascetics traced all mortal pleasure to the single root of sex, and set about eradicating it. They found it exceedingly tough and suited their methods to the task.

The monastic authorities discountenanced ascetic excesses no more successfully than the diocesan authorities had once tried to bridle monasticism itself. The popular appeal, first of monasticism and then of ascetic excesses, was too extensive to permit effectual disciplinary measures. An early wave of mass self-castrations in the Eastern hotbed of heresies ebbed as it was allied with theological deviation; however, where ascetic practice went along with orthodox theory it was hard to put down.

How would you punish men whose self-punishment left nothing to be added save the merciful release of death? How could you deny them special sanctity, much less excommunicate them, when all the world was lost in admiration of them? Sainthood became peculiarly associated with asceticism. Egocentric immolation superseded humanitarian sacrifice.

Hermits donned iron shackles, chains, barbed girdles and spiked collars, hair shirts, or went about without any clothes at all; they had themselves flogged insensible or tied up in, one would have thought, impossible positions. St Simeon Stylites (c. 390–459), archetype of the pillar monks whom his example continued to inspire for over a thousand years, was the first to achieve solitary confinement in public. He had a pillar built, low at first but gradually increased in height to sixty feet, on which he lived for thirty-six years until his demise. There he received pilgrims and dispensed instruction and advice every afternoon, meanwhile feeding maggots on his self-inflicted wounds which he kept open for that purpose. 'Eat what God has given you!' he chid a worm that fell off, and put it back.

Imitators of Simeon were ordained to the priesthood on their lofty, noisome perches, celebrated mass, prayed over the sick brought to them below, and gave consultations to popes and emperors. One holy man crouched in a hanging barrel for ten years, others rolled in thorns and nettles, deliberately attracted insect bites, burnt themselves with fire and irritated their injuries to chronic purulence. A starvation diet being a matter of course, some improved on this by eating only rotten or otherwise disgusting food, others by inducing prolonged constipation. Some spent weeks and months immersed in foul or icy water, some never washed at all, some made arrangements so that they could never sit or lie down.

On towering platforms, on level ground, in cellars, in desert caves or in the market places, there was no end to the inventiveness of these saintly persons. Only a few threw in their hands and fled into extremes of hyperaesthesia where all manifestations of physical existence, including light, were alike insupportably painful, retiring into a semi-cataleptic semblance to the disembodied state. Nearly all these people survived for decades under conditions that would quickly kill if imposed from outside.

And all the time the thing that plagued them most was aggravated. The more rigorously they fought the root evil of lust, the more lustily it spread itself in them. Preoccupation with lust engendered lust in the unlikeliest quarters, distilled it from the most far-fetched sources, and maintained it at constant boiling point. Never in the most licentious pagan societies had eroticism flourished so feverishly. After a time the luckless puritans thought of virtually nothing else but sex. Even on their death beds (very often in extreme old age), emaciated, covered with running sores, crusted with the grime of years and worn out by every possible sort of hardship, saints often testified that concupiscence was still alive in them, and kicking. It was with erotic fantasies rather than intellectual doubts that Satan would tempt the saint in his dying hour – when a lifetime of piety was set at naught if the poor moribund fell from grace at the last and gave in to his desires even if only in the abstract.

But once he was safely dead, his spirit safely out of reach of the wiles of evil, the material ballast left behind him was contradictorily appropriated by the living for their spiritual uplift. Relics – a term once merely denoting the effects of a deceased person, and a commodity once merely cherished for reasons of sentiment and loyalty – had come to be credited with active virtue. The remains of a saint, or objects which had been in intimate contact with him, were held to be charged with a portion of his holiness. Such relics were at once serviceable foci for devotional concentration, strengthening medicine for those yet labouring under the disease of life, and means of getting in touch with the departed saint – metaphorically tugging at his sleeve – to solicit his patronage.

As the charred bones of St Polycarp had been reverently gathered up (in the first documented instance of this practice), as the flock of St Cyprian of Carthage had spread cloths to soak up his blood for keeping when he was beheaded, as ever since the discovery of the True Cross people had been wearing splinters of it set in jewellery – so now buried martyr's bones were dug up for edifying exhibition and amulets containing fragmentary relics were all the rage. Matters went so far that presently the bodies of persons liable to come up for canonisation were sometimes scarcely allowed to cool before pious deathbed vultures fell upon the fresh corpse to take it to pieces for general distribution, with unseemly wrangling afterwards as to the relative value of the parts, and disputes regarding the authenticity of mysteriously multiplied organs. A regular traffic in relics grew up, expanding constantly with the development of pilgrimage.

This development followed a very similar pattern. People at first only wanted to see the sites of the Passion and other holy places, for atmosphere and a better grasp of the relevant events. By degrees it began to be felt that active virtue emanated from the hallowed ground. To have made such a journey became more than a pious pleasure, it became a spiritual health cure, and after that a meritorious act. It became a status feature, a penitential exercise, a means of winning heavenly favours; and sacred souvenirs acquired on the spot naturally appeared all the more precious and potent.

There were all too many sites sanctified by Christian martyrdom, and shrines sprang up everywhere, usually incorporating relics, and increasingly endowed in the public mind with wonder-working powers. The distinction between supplicating for a saint's prayers on high, and praying to the saint, blurred. The distinction blurred, too, between addressing the saint through the token of his former existence and addressing that token as a vital agent in its own right. And the distinction between doing something for one's self by acts of devotion and doing something for the deity by way of adoration, practically disappeared.

Church Fathers, Doctors, bishops, abbots, thoughtful priests issued repeated warnings against the implicit dangers they perceived, of the three prime factors of paganism – idolatry, magic, and trading with the deity – coming to adulterate the faith. Repeatedly they stressed the distinctions: a relic was something to be honoured, not worshipped, an amulet was a wholesome trinket, not a talisman, God bestowed his blessings from sheer mercy not in return for services rendered, the saints and angels in heaven were not to be regarded as friends at court, only as examples and counsellors. But it was difficult even for intellectually wide-awake minds to hold fast to these principles all the time. The whole idea of sacrifice, redemption, atonement, and reward too easily translated itself into terms of human commerce.

Useless to rely on the intellect, when human reason and divine rationale were entirely disparate media. Better to abandon ratiocination, abdicate cerebral activity altogether in relation to matters of faith.

The burning of the martyrs

Reason had its part in ethics and conduct, but heaven was to be comprehended only in mystic rapture beyond articulate expression.

The saints had already forsworn property, ease, pleasures, and independent will; now the intellectual faculties themselves were added to the range of expendable encumbrances. What has been called the under-witted saint made his début: the holy simpleton whose total surrender to God was in no way obstructed by irrelevant mental machinery having to be got out of the way. Reason and self-expression were, of course, still required to exhort, explain, and minister; but theologians, priests, princes and the people all prostrated themselves to the human vessels of pure, artless goodness and grace.

Though assuredly the Sermon on the Mount had not been directed at the unthinking, 'Blessed are the poor in spirit' had become its sovereign burden for the present. The supreme endeavour of the saintly mind now was to efface and cancel itself out. From the egalitarian brotherhood of believers in a universal, unmaterial diffusion of sanctity, there had crystallised another pantheon, wherein the most holy under God approximated the most closely to idols, that is, insentient receptacles of numinous virtue and material obeisance.

9
Woman

Women played a distinguished part in the growth of Christianity.
Wherever he preached, numbers of women followed Jesus. Wherever
he stopped during his itinerant ministry, women figured prominently
among his hosts and among those who by their faith in him received
healing. Considering the inferior position, as regards both civil status
and spiritual estimation, of women under Jewish law, surprisingly many
are mentioned by name and depicted as persons of mettle in the Gospel:
beginning with Peter's mother-in-law whom Jesus cured of fever and
ending with the Samaritan woman whom he actually despatched to her
village as his herald.

Jesus clearly made no distinctions of sex between human beings; he
spoke to women just as to anybody else and as readily let them speak to
him. Rather than speak for themselves, the sons of Zebedee put their
mother up to asking him to take them on as his special lieutenants; the
sisters Martha and Mary did not hesitate to draw him into their little
family squabble; he took the trouble to save a delinquent chattel like
the woman taken in adultery and raised up another, defiled by prosti-
tution, to walk with him. The Canaanite woman, the woman suffering
from haemorrhages, the daughter of Jairus, Susanna, Joanna, Salome,
Mary the wife of Cleophas – the very fact that they appeared in all four
of the official gospels is significant.

A whole troop of women crossed into Judaea with Jesus from
Galilee, the housewives of Jerusalem spread their carpets and greenery
for him on Palm Sunday; with the one exception of John only the
women of Jesus' inner circle dared to show themselves at the foot of the
cross. The first person to whom he manifested his resurrection was a
woman, and that woman the same Mary of Magdala who had used to
live basely by the professional exploitation of her womanhood. He had
even allowed himself to be born of woman in the ordinary way – 'inter
sanguinem et faeces', amid blood and faeces, as St Augustine would

brutally describe the process in the bitterness of his own revulsion from the common mode of origin. But although by then Jesus' submission to that process would be counted as an additional instance of the sacrificial indignities he had embraced, there was no suggestion of that kind either in Jesus' lifetime or in the teachings of the apostles. Neither the act of generation nor its issue of parturition were expressly execrated, the womb was not yet by definition an object of distaste.

Couples, not merely the male heads of households, were listed among the property owners who gave their possessions to the first Christian community in Jerusalem after Jesus' death, among the first Christian synagogues in Greek territory, and also at Rome. The institution of deacons was augmented by deaconesses. Paul the bachelor for all his aura of cerebral austerity, brought in strong reinforcements of women converts. Women were the keenest church-goers, as they were to be through the ages. The first Gentile congregations evidently showed a preponderance of women, and women accordingly formed a large percentage of those early martyrs that compose more than half of the existing canon.

The weaker sex evinced the most spectacular strength during the persecutions, winning untold proselytes with its example. The modern mind, even when it does not shrink from contemplating atrocities that beggar the imagination, does not feel elevated by them either – the reason being that in our time the element of deliberate testimony, and so of triumphal glory, has been lacking from such acts. They have been acts on the part of the perpetrators, for which the victims may be pitied, mourned, respected – but scarcely envied. The crowded roll of females of all ages and classes, from little girls to crones, from slaves to patricians, who were martyred for the Christian faith, was not seen as a cenotaph of victims but rather a gallery of conquerors whose vulnerable constitution enhanced their greatness.

Not a few Fathers of the Church were the sons of strong-minded Christian mothers. It has to be remembered that even when Christianity had become a licensed, state religion, people were not born into it but entered of their own decision. Only a minority did so in their nonage; as a rule baptism was a rite for adults. The eight principal Doctors, with the possible exception of Basil, received baptism as mature men; with the exception of Hilary, who was of pagan parentage, they all paid tribute to the religious influence on them of their mothers. With no exception, they took a strong ascetic line against sex and its epitome, the womb.

Partly no doubt the galloping trend of identifying evil-matter-lust dogmatically with the 'insatiable concupiscence of woman', was due to a reaction against the flamboyant sexuality of the southern and oriental pagan cultures and against the priapic rites which were an inalienable part of pagan pantheism. However, the conclusion is hard to avoid that it was fostered by the psychological idiosyncrasies of the leading exponents of dogma during the formative period between 200 and 450. The most important of the early theologians, Origen (c. 185–254), emasculated himself ('a step he afterwards regretted'), in order to render himself fit for teaching women; another uncanonised Greek Father, Clement of Alexandria, shifted the onus, directing that 'every woman should blush at the thought that she is a woman'. St Jerome was more candid when explaining to a critic why he was so determined on prescribing celibacy: 'You, who fight [carnal temptation] may either conquer or be conquered. I who run away shall not be conquered, since I flee from the enemy; and the reason why I flee is that I may not be conquered.' As simple as that.

Where the prescription came too late St Jerome contented himself with, 'he who too ardently loves his own wife is an adulterer'. Eustathius of Antioch exhorted husbands to leave their wives and women to dress like men, that it might be as far as possible forgotten they existed. St John Chrysostom, 'the golden-mouthed', had this to say to persons contemplating marriage: 'The groundwork of corporeal beauty is nothing else but phlegm and blood and slime and bile and the fluids of masticated food . . . When you see a rag with any of these on it, you cannot bear to touch it even with the tips of your fingers, nay, you cannot bear to look at it. How then can you be in a flutter of excitement about the storehouses of these things?' How, indeed? In the unavailing effort to convince humankind that the living sum of 'these things' had really nothing more to it than the single components, saints of this calibre took to wallowing in them. Thus, without prejudice to their own chastity, they might possibly succeed in redeeming the world from lust, by vicarious suffering, just as Jesus' death had redeemed the world unto eternal life.

St Jerome, shown here in an edition of his *Epistles*, printed in 1497

No trace of these extravagances appeared until the second century. St Paul, like Jesus, clearly had not felt unduly troubled by the flesh, and while virginity and abstinence were recognised as spiritual muscle-builders, they were not magnified into absolute concomitants of holiness for several generations. It was distinctly a post-apostolic contribution to the Christian outlook. Was the sweeping revolt against the flesh in any way compensatory, to vent men's chagrin that the older, easier values of pagan ethic had gone by the board? the back-handed revenge of the deposed gods, rationalised? Had any of the vehement ascetics, perhaps, suffered shipwreck on their first youthful ventures in love? The scope of speculation is unlimited. But while nothing is so dangerous to judgment as snap generalisation, the saints in question themselves plunged headlong into that very pitfall. Before many more generations had gone by, the progressive formula evil = matter = lust = woman swamped everything.

In a pre-scientific age, no calamity was ever 'natural' but the result of direct supernatural machinations. Death itself, whether by violence or sickness, had no 'natural causes' but resulted from supernatural intervention of one sort or another: when it was not the will of God, it was witchcraft. Witchcraft was the magic of the Devil enacted through his human agents: so now witchcraft also stemmed from Woman, and with it all earthly ills and perils – not excluding imperfections and malpractices within Church and state. Theological thought pivoted on the horrid crux, it was the fulcrum of social critique, the hub of morality, and of course the ultimate substance of original sin. Common humanity, incapable of making the grade of total abstention, lusted and sinned away forthrightly as ever, but yet yielded to the constant ideological pressure and accepted the ruling standard. Soon perpetual virginity would be enough by itself to make a saint.

But simultaneously quite another development was taking shape.

In order that Jesus be resurrected it was necessary for him to have become man and died in the flesh, wherefore it was necessary for him to be born of woman. It was necessary for the woman honoured with the task of giving birth to him, to be without sin, and since the nuclear area of sin had shrunk to the act of generation, she must be absolutely cleared of this. Initially to combat the Arian Heresy which represented Jesus as a creature, not an uncreate aspect of the deity, the miracle of the immaculate conception needed to be thoroughly consolidated. The virgin birth, which previously had been as it were incidental, now became a cornerstone of dogma. St Augustine's binding dictum, 'As regards the mother of God, I will not allow any question whatsoever of sin', became by degrees extended beyond the maternal role of the Virgin Mary. It was finally ruled that by a unique divine dispensation she herself had been conceived immaculate, that is, without the universal human heritage from Adam and Eve, of original sin.

This, now, put the Virgin Mary in a class by herself. She was not divine, but she was not properly human either, unlike the saints who had one and all had to slough off original sin. In her, the womb, that origin of evil, was the origin of the highest good. It had to be admitted that if, 'from a woman came our destruction', then also, 'from a woman came our salvation'. By virtue of motherhood the Virgin was holier than any other virgins. She was the Queen of Heaven.

Christianity had raised the female soul to equality with the male soul. Once humanity thus ceased to be an all-male species, an all-male Trinity was not enough. The women who composed so solid an element of the congregations wanted to be catered for, and made their mark upon the cultus. Religious art might depict Lust, Vanity and the Serpent in female form, but it gave female form also to Piety, Charity, Wisdom, and for that matter 'Mother' Church. More: answering the chronic human incapacity of belief in a wholly merciful and loving God (seeing that after every access of softening the divine persona, worshippers relapse into grooming their God for the part of a vengeful tyrant) – Love and Mercy, those key factors of the Christian creed, became peculiarly the preserve of Christ's gentle mother.

The Mary-cult, which eventually set up images to motherhood with all its earthly trappings – including lactation and diapers – as objects of immediate veneration, was an outstanding case in point of doctrine having to catch up with popular practice.

For inevitably the cult of Mary reflected on her sex, so that the womb paradoxically became sanctified in accomplishing its carnal function, the very function which had brought it into disrepute. In course of time it would be postulated that the female sex was the better part of mankind and indeed the model of a coming, superior stage of human evolution. Peter Abelard, who formulated this, in fact went so far as to allot first place among saints to the Magdalen, the reformed handmaiden of the principle of lust. Again, unwittingly he ratified a *fait accompli* of popular devotion: for in the Middle Ages the cult of the fair penitent ranked second only to that of the Virgin Mary, saving the Holy Trinity.

10

The Saintly Code

Other creeds owned priests, priest-kings, deified monarchs, magicians, or fabulous chimerae. The saint as distinct from any of those categories was a unique creation of Christianity. Of attested human origin, he formed the missing link between man and God, at once mediator and buffer. That some saints have turned out to be mythical does not alter the fact that as a genus saints rose from the ranks of actual, living human beings. They thus reinforced the crucial humanity of the risen Messiah. Little though we know with any certainty about Mithraism, a cult which during the first three centuries of our era ran neck and neck with Christianity in many parts of Europe and the Near East and had a number of similar features, it seems likely that its kindred attractions were ultimately offset by the emphatically historic Christ as against the frankly mythological Mithras.

The ideal of saintliness, as immanent in the falling short of it as in attainment, suffused the whole civilisation which it came to dominate. People believed in it even when it was beyond them. To the best of men's belief it was holiness – not birth, not wealth, nor strength and power, but holiness alone – which determined the structure of Christian society. The apex of society was not the ruler but the saint. The body politic and the sacral realm had separated, yet the priesthood stood above secular aristocracy and in turn bowed to the saint whatever his original walk of life. Prelates humbled themselves to simple monks and kings submitted to the oracular judgment of anchorites knowing less than nothing of affairs, so long as those innocents stood in the odour of sanctity by popular acclaim. For the saint was also the most vocal member of society, and the most eminent in the public eye. He supplied the only social services there were, provider, nurse, and beggar for the needy, counsellor and good example. Although at heart a non-conformist, and therefore usually a thorn in the side of government whether temporal or ecclesiastical, the saint set the prevailing standard of conformity to the herd-wish for 'belonging'.

The Martyrdom of St Katherine. The legend is that Katherine's refusal to deny her faith led to her being tortured on a spiked wheel which, however, miraculously fell to pieces. Drawing by Lelio Orsi.

Christ between two martyrs, a fourth-century fresco from the catacomb of Commodilla, Rome.

Fresco of Innocent I from the old Basilica of St Paolo. Innocent was Pope from 402 to 417. According to an anecdote related by his successor Zosimus, Innocent gave permission for prayer and sacrifices to pagan deities during the siege of Rome by the Goths (408), when plague, famine and despair were rampant.

Ivory disk of unknown date found in the catacombs of St Sebastiano, Rome. Note the martyr's palm branch on the left.

The Virgin Mary with a
collection of infant saints.
From a Flemish screen painting
in Ranworth Church, Norfolk.

Gregory the Great, Pope and scholar, born in Rome *c.* 540, pontiff from
590 to 604. He brought about reform in the administration of the Roman
Church and was for centuries a source of inspiration to Western clergy.
Painting by Saraceni. Note the loving attempt at naturalistic
characterisation in a wholly imaginary portrait. The tiara of his office rests
aside, while all the time the Holy Spirit hovers by him.

At the same time, however, intrinsic sanctity continued to attach to worldly rank. As God, right at the summit, was the only fount of holiness, holiness descended the social scale by accurate degrees. Fealty, fidelity and faith remained as closely related conceptually as they were etymologically. The king commanded supreme fealty and therefore a higher degree of holiness than did lesser lords, and so on down to the bottom, where there was – materially speaking – none. So while in theory worldly position might not in itself amount to anything, in practice it happened that, on the whole, spiritual and mundane status overlapped. If humility and dispossession were the earthly hallmark of heavenly affluence, while yet authority and pomp remained the properties of sovereign power, how was that contradiction to be resolved?

The solution was to hand. It lay in the saintly transposition of realities, which turned the whole cosmos inside out.

Since true reality was only in the sphere of the unseen and un-material, the tangible world was a mere reflection of it. All earthly events were merely variations on a charade forever spelling out the divine synopsis. Nothing on earth, therefore, was what it seemed; no thing was essentially itself, but first and foremost a symbol of something else – something pertaining to the spiritual world. No earthly object or action but was a unit in the comprehensive alphabet of Christian symbolism.

Take an apple. The apple was a reminder of the original sin of Adam and Eve. But it also exemplified the beautiful order in which the divine architect had constructed the universe. Furthermore, in eating an apple one might simultaneously honour and mimic the deity: by consuming three quarters for the Trinity and the fourth in remembrance of the love with which Mary gave her child Jesus an apple to eat. In that connection, the last quarter should be left unpeeled, as little boys do not peel their apples, while immediately after Christmas the last quarter should not be eaten at all, since a new-born infant cannot eat apples. Thus the fruit was many things – a call to repentance, an earnest of corruption, a stimulant of joy in God, and a means of homoeopathic worship, to name only a selection. The only thing it was not, was simply an apple. In the climate of total allegory, an object defined only by certain physical properties but lacking ulterior implications soon came to elude mental grasp.

While it would be over-optimistic to attribute a full understanding of so elaborate a code alphabet to the mass of humanity, this was not for want of trying. The saints showed how the devout imagination could turn the most ordinary everyday routine into a Passion play. Thus there was drama and colour in the most grinding occupations, to be had for the tapping – while conversely high adventure might be a mime symbolic of plodding submission, all the time.

In the same way, then, worldly power, wealth, authority became mere semblances, celebrating in sign language the glories of worldly abnegation. The panoply of greatness represented the triumph of lowliness, in code. Man at long last achieved his desire of having his cake and eating it – provided he remembered always to make a meaningful ceremony of the procedure.

Religious exposition indeed drew copiously on alimentary metaphor – terms that surely everyone must understand. God was 'a greedy glutton with a voracious appetite: he devours even the marrow of our bones', and was himself likened to a good meal. 'You will eat him, roasted at the fire, baked to a turn, neither underdone nor burnt.' Christ's thirsty love of our souls was just like the drunkard's obsession.

The glutton and the drunkard thus could at a pinch claim to be miming the love of God; a juicy cut off the joint might be relished as an image of spiritual nutrition. Feasting and fasting could be practically the same. And when the union of Christ and his Church was held to mirror the carnal marriage bond, carnal marriage became somewhat rehabilitated. Life on earth had to go on, and saintliness had to adjust or resign. By virtue of unflagging symbological adaptation, the ideal in fact kept its grip on the wayward world.

But symbolic inversion once set going could go on for ever, re-inverting itself. With the intention of spiritualising the material object, the spiritual object being made intelligible through sensuous apprehension became tied down to the material representation. Indirectly the saint was responsible for the development of Christian religious art, whereby the adamant, anti-idolatrous Mosaic embargo on 'graven images' was lifted – or rather, was completely reversed.

It was in the catacombs, the graveyard maquis of the Primitive Church, that this process began.

'I believe there were good Christians – once,' St Jerome said sourly, 'In the age of the catacombs . . .' He was not so far removed from that age, and as a schoolboy often made excursions into the gloomy labyrinths that had his approval. Had he never noticed the wall paintings down there?

Saintliness was relative, even then. 'You do well to beat your breast with that stone,' Pope Sixtus v apostrophised a picture of St Jerome, some twelve hundred years later. 'Without it you would never have been numbered among the saints.'

The most irascible and vituperative of Christian writers, Jerome was in truth a saint *honoris causa*, canonised for scholarship rather than the more customary marks of holiness (his furious chastity apart): and St Jerome in all probability would have hurled his stone at his painted portrait. He, like nearly all the early Church Fathers, deprecated representational art and considered graphic rendering of sacred themes a profanation. Their predecessors had gloried in the classical accusation brought against Jews and Christians alike, of atheism on the grounds that they eschewed all visible aids to devotion; and successors of theirs for centuries to come renewed the attempt to stifle the heathenish aberration. In Gentile Christendom, that proved impossible. The Graeco-Roman mentality could scarcely conceive of life without representational art, much less of religion; and the martyr saints of the catacomb age constituted the thin end of the wedge.

At first only symbols had been allowed for sacred decorations – objects definitely illustrating things other than themselves, like the lamb of purity, the ox of sacrifice, the pictorial pun of the fish, and so on. The cross, which although symbolic of the Passion actually signified a cross, hardly appeared in the beginning, when, too, there was of course no question of portraying Christ any more than God the Father. But as the toll of martyrs grew ever heavier, their brethren succumbed to the temptation of commemorating them and their sufferings in pictures. (Christ joined the company in the guise – one might almost say the disguise, of the Good Shepherd, looking not unlike a pastoral Dionysos: that is to say, *a quality* of the Saviour was shown, and not the Saviour himself.) No worship was involved – but then, there was as yet no hagiolatry at that time. Worship of saints entered later, bringing with it that inevitable confusion of image and reality, symbol and truth, which caused so much grave concern among the ecclesiastical leadership.

By the beginning of the fourth century images of saints and timid pictorial allusions to the Trinity had emerged above ground, on the walls of churches and in the lararial niches of private houses. They were forbidden and removed from time to time, to reappear after decent intervals. Bible manuscripts began to blossom with illumination, and the recurrence of church decrees now ordering destruction of frescos and hangings which depicted holy personages revealed how rife they were.

Churches had come out of hiding with a vengeance. Now they were everywhere the towering landmarks of the community, and following the lead of Emperor Constantine Christendom strove to make them as much akin to palaces as possible. Where once the Lord's Supper had been celebrated clandestinely on a coffin top, now it was surrounded with the most exquisite and precious artefacts, and relics of the saints were mounted in luxurious splendour. Nobody would gainsay that it was pious to adorn God's altars; but adornment inexorably grew more representational rather than less, in the form of murals, mosaics and stained glass, larger than life and many times as glowing. Pope Gregory the Great at last gave a characteristically realistic verdict: while pictures and statues certainly must not be worshipped, it was equally wrong to destroy them once they had been placed inside a house of God. 'What those who can read learn by means of writing, that do the uneducated learn by looking at a picture.' Christianity when it went among the Barbarians had ceased to be *ipso facto* literate. The church was on its way towards becoming the 'visual Bible of the people'.

So far, so good – but that was not the end of the matter. In the East the battle of the second commandment renewed itself at frequent intervals throughout the ensuing two hundred years, waxing more violent at every fresh outbreak, until iconoclasm ceased to affect only images and became a byword for ferocious civil war and tyranny. It was largely Western revulsion from this which paved the way for the ultimate division of the Greek from the Roman-oriented churches. In the West, henceforth, religious art never looked back. For a thousand years it monopolised human creative endeavour.

The saints offered unending subject matter. It took time for the

artist to lose his shyness *vis-à-vis* the deity. God the Father might
at most be hinted at by the picture of a hand or an eye – tentatively
humanised but so far still nonetheless strictly symbolic. The Holy
Spirit, hardest of numinous aspects to comprehend, had been seen by
John the Baptist to descend on Jesus 'like a dove'; so a dove it was –
notwithstanding the bird's close association with the unconquerable
goddess, Venus. As for the Christ, reverence dictated treating the
Passion as a metaphysical formality, so that at first he was shown only
in unmoved, inhuman, carefully stereotyped majesty – dispensing
catharsis of terror without the pity – often with his court of saints.

Once again the saints came forward for the human interest. To
start with they, too, were shown uniformly stylised, wearing the in-
signia of their martyrdoms or of the most captivating incidents of their
lives, for identification.

Thus St Bartholomew would carry his own skin and the knife with
which he had been flayed, St Lawrence the gridiron on which he had
been roasted, St Katherine the spiked wheel to which she had been
tied, St Clement the anchor tied around his neck for drowning, St
Simon Zealot the saw used in dismembering him, St Stephen the stones
and St James the Less the club or fuller's bat with which they had respectively been killed. On the other hand, St Barbara's attributes were
a tower with three windows or a peacock's feather – the first in reference
to her conversion, the second in reference to her birthplace, Heliopolis,
the city of the phoenix – a bird to which the peacock served as the
nearest Western equivalent. St Joseph had his carpenter's tools or a
budded staff connected with his legendary courtship of the Virgin;
the physician brothers, St Cosmas and St Damian, had the dress and
adjuncts of their trade; St Ambrose bore a scourge in token of his zeal
against the Arians (or sometimes a beehive, because of a pretty story
that a swarm of bees had settled on his infant lips, presaging future
eloquence); St James the Great bore the scallop shell, gourd, and
staff of pilgrimage; St Euphemia was accompanied by the bear which
had *not* devoured her, St Agnes by an entirely symbolic lamb.

But so had St John Baptist got a lamb as an alternative to his own
head on a salver; often several different saints bore variants of the
same hieratic crest. The lion was a favourite: St Jerome, St Mark,
St Mary of Egypt, St Paul the Hermit, and St Onuphrius (who had

The head of John the Baptist is borne to Salome

two) were among those who shared that beast; St Philip, St Sylvester
St Margaret of Antioch and St Martha shared the dragon with St
George. St Martha also had keys for an emblem, though not crossed
like those of St Peter; the cross and the sword were attached to numbers
of saints, as were the holy dove, a loaf or loaves of bread, and pen and
inkhorn to those who had wielded the implements of literature with
distinction. So when it was a matter of narrative rather than devotional
images, some more personal characterisation began to be desired.
Admittedly this was only one of many contributory factors which led
to the next departure in the direction of pre-Christian realism in art:
but at all events the saints lent themselves to the first experiments in
that direction.

While a rigid formalism fettered the religious art of eastern Christendom for evermore, in the west Nature encroached by leaps and bounds
upon the domain of supernatural representation. People believed the
more firmly in beings whose real existence was made more and more
credible in circumstantial verisimilitude of delineation; people worshipped the more seriously the more the object of worship was made
to resemble the profane real-thing. The artist and his public, like God
when he had made the material world, stepped back and 'saw that it was
good', after all.

Beauty was no longer a snare and a delusion, but once again the
best proof of the divinity of Creation; it should not be spurned but
praised. Particular images as well as particular relics now were capable
of working miracles and became endowed with individual personalities
apart from the soul-units bearing their names which were in heaven.
An image as well as a person could become a saint.

Scenes from the lives of realistically fashioned saints demanded
realistic settings. As soon as saints were shown not merely ranged in
ceremonial stance around the heavenly throne but in action cheek by
jowl with ordinary mortals, it became necessary to distinguish them
that they should be instantly recognisable. A field of radiance emanating
from the holy person came into use, and by degrees evolved into several
standard forms: the halo, usually circular, placed behind the head;
the aureole, a zone of light framing the whole figure; the glory, a
combination of the two; and the mandorla, a glory enclosed in an oval,
which was reserved to Jesus and Mary, just as the triangular nimbus,

A female orans with dove from the catacombs of Domitalli, Rome

signifying the Trinity, was reserved to God the Father. Occasionally a nimbus in the symbolically inferior geometric shape of the square was given to a person still among the living, in complimentary antici-pation. The wheel had come full circle. Humanity was elevated to holiness, and the holy was brought down to earth again.

More especially through the cult of the Virgin mother, the human rather than the divine nature of the Saviour came to be increasingly stressed. The crucified Jesus began to suffer; his image became over-whelmingly identified with pain: his living reality was asserted pre-dominantly in his death. Pity rejoined terror as a constituent of spiritual purgation.

But the trouble with pity is that it is chiefly an imaginative projection of self-pity. Adam had re-made God in *his* image, fully; and familiarity, they say, breeds contempt. Insensibly the decline of absolute faith was ushered in.

The saint of painting and sculpture, a creature so convincingly like you and me, could no longer wear an old-style halo, which against a naturalistic background looked too much like some ludicrous headgear. The solid-gold disk, stuck, as it were, on the back of the head, became attenuated into a thin circlet of light which, for good measure, floated in perspective, *above* the head. But thus paradoxically the halo became for its part a 'real' object, rather than a pictographic shorthand sign. By tacit assumption in the popular mind, a saint was a person who had a golden hoop that followed him about.

And thus the final paradox: the saint, a humble, flesh and blood sectary by origin, in his apotheosis became unreal; and reality drained steadily away from what he stood for. Faith itself became incredible, requiring strenuous imaginative exercises for its maintenance. Only the ethical yardstick, which the saint had been instrumental in furnishing, stayed plain and stark. A saint, at least, was a good man.

An ideal by definition is a thing unrealised, a goal which to retain its lure must remain always unattainable, if only just. The uniquely Christian ideal of altruistic love and service coupled with a bounden missionary duty – for better or for worse, and sometimes in admittedly bizarre extensions – is what made the climate of the world we know.

Notes on further reading

Augustine, Saint: *The Confessions of St Augustine*, tr. F. J. Sheed, 1943.

Barrett, C. K.: *The New Testament Background: Selected Documents*, 1956.

Bede, the Venerable: *A History of the English Church and People*, tr. L. Sherley-Price, 1955.

Bruce, F. F.: *The Spreading Flame*, 1958.

Butler, Alban: *Butler's Lives of the Saints*, ed. H. Thurston and D. Attwater, 1956.

Daniel-Rops, H.: *The Church of Apostles and Martyrs*, 1960.

Daniel-Rops, M.: *Jesus in His Time*, 1955.

Delahaye, H.: *The Legends of the Saints*, 1962.

Eusebius: *The Ecclesiastical History*, Loeb Class. Lib.

Harnak, A.: *Die Mission und Ausbreitung des Christentums in den ersten Jahrhunderten*, 1916.

Hughes, P.: *A History of the Church*, 1948.

Josephus, Flavius: *Works*, Loeb Class. Lib.

Latourete, K. S.: *A History of Christianity*, 1954.

Prat, F.: *The Theology of St Paul*, 1957.

Index